The Incredible Battle of Castle Itter:

© 2023 by Len Sandler

ISBN: 9798363279225

Cover photo courtesy Steve J. Morgan, WC, (CC-by-SA 3.0)

Table of Contents

Chapter	Pg.
1. The Beginning of the End	1
2. The Setting	12
3. The Handyman	30
4. The Suicide & the Escape	40
5. The Waffen-SS Captain	46
6. The Cook & the Wehrmacht Major	53
7. The American Captain	62
8. Preparing for Battle	75
9. The Battle	78
10. The Tennis Player	95
11. The War is Over	112
"The Last Battle"	127

Dedication

This book is dedicated to the memory of our son Craig who fought a courageous battle of his own. Unfortunately, the good guys don't always win.

Ch. 1 – The Beginning of the End

Austrian by birth, Adolph Hitler was a high school drop-out who aspired to be an artist. He, however, was twice rejected after applying for admission to the Vienna Academy of Fine Arts. Unable to pay rent on his apartment, he landed in a homeless shelter when he was 20 years old. On November 9, 1923 he lead an angry Nazi party mob that marched from Bürgerbräukeller, a beer hall in Munich, to the Bavarian War Ministry in a failed attempt to overthrow the government. Sixteen rioters and four police officers were killed in what became known as the "Beer Hall Putsch."

Hitler was arrested, tried for treason, and sentenced to five years in Landsberg Prison. Pardoned by the Bavarian Supreme Court in a controversial decision, he was released on December 20, 1924, against the state prosecutor's objections. Including time on remand, he wound up being confined for just over a year.

Shortly before Hitler was eligible for parole, the Bavarian government attempted to have him sent back to Austria. The Federal Chancellor at the time, Ignaz Seipel, rejected the request on the grounds that his service in the German Army during World War I voided his Austrian citizenship. In truth, Austria had recognized the citizenship of other German soldiers and Seipel simply didn't want Hitler back in Austria. In response, Hitler angrily renounced his citizenship. It was likely not a coincidence that Austria was the first country that the Führer chose to make part of his Third Reich after assuming control of the German government.

On March 12, 1938, Austria was taken over by Nazi Germany in what became known as the *Anschluss* or "Annexation." Hitler wanted to unite all ethnic German territories and Austria was the first step in his dream of establishing a Third Reich that would last for a thousand years. Hitler believed, and convinced many, that he was on a divine mission. In his hometown of Linz, Austria later that year, he proclaimed:

> "I believe it was the will of God to send a boy from here into the Reich, to make him great, to raise him up to be Führer of the nation." 1

Adolph Hitler
Photo courtesy Bundesarchiv, Bild 183-H1216-0500-002 / CC-BY-SA

At first, then Chancellor Kurt Schuschnigg indicated he wanted to hold a national referendum for the people to decide whether or not they wanted to become part of Germany. Before the vote could be held, however, the Austrian Nazi Party seized power in a coup d'état. The new Pro-Nazi government in Vienna declared Austria to be annexed by Nazi Germany.

The so-called "referendum" was held less than a month after the Anschluss. Austrians were asked whether they supported the union that had already taken place with Germany. It was well-known that the Nazis recorded how each person cast a ballot. Anyone objecting to the German occupation would likely face an unpleasant interview with the Gestapo and be subject to a mysterious disappearance. The outcome was a not-too-surprising 99.7% of the people in favor of continuing to abandon Austrian independence.

The German war effort hinged on assimilating soldiers from each conquered country. Austria was no exception. Within days of the take-over, the entire Austrian army was absorbed by the Germans. This produced mixed results. Some Austrians served willingly. Some were even enthusiastic about it. But others accepted orders only as a last resort in order to stay alive. German groups tried to weed out anyone who was a potential threat to them. In many of the countries taken over by Germany during World War II, soldiers who did not believe in the Nazi cause still ended up in their ranks.

The Waffen-SS had actually been operating in Austria since 1934 with the intent of identifying anyone whose loyalty to the Third Reich could be questioned. Dissidents, nationalists, leftists, communists and many others were rounded up and imprisoned.

Following the fall of Paris on June 14, 1940, Vichy was made the capital of the unoccupied areas of France. The Nazis had direct control in occupied France and the Pétain government in Vichy was granted semiautonomous governing powers in unoccupied France. With the Germans keeping a watchful eye on them, Pétain's government cooperated extensively with the Germans.

Between 1939 and 1941, Germany invaded and occupied a number of other countries including Poland, Norway, Denmark, Netherlands, Belgium, Luxembourg, Greece, Yugoslavia, and Italy.

It took seven years and the greatest death toll from any war in history but on March 22, 1945, Allied troops finally pushed across the Rhine River, advancing deep into Germany from the west. On April 20, the Soviets launched their final offensive from the east against the Nazi capital of Berlin. Severely under-resourced, the Germans had no hope of holding off the Allies.

Hitler confined himself to his Berlin bunker where he would meet only with his inner circle of loyalists. As he wallowed in self-pity, he blamed military officers for their incompetence and the German people themselves for a lack of determination. On April 30, he committed suicide inside his underground bunker in Berlin as the Germans and Soviets fought a bloody urban battle in the streets above. On May 2, Berlin fell to the Russians and the war was all but lost.

As is typical in democracies, soldiers in pre-Nazi Germany had to swear an oath to uphold the constitution and state legal institutions.

After the Nazis took power, however, soldier were required to take a new oath: "I swear to God this holy oath that I shall render unconditional obedience to the Leader of the German Reich and people, Adolf Hitler, Supreme Commander of the Armed forces."

Unprecedented in any modern European country, the oath required a pledge of allegiance toward a single individual and not to the state. While Hitler was alive, many Germans were ready to fight to the end because of the oath. After the Fuhrer's suicide, though, some German soldiers considered that their pledge had died with him. They didn't feel the same willingness to fight to the bitter end.

Why did Hitler kill himself? In one of his more prescient quotes, he once said, "If you win, you need not have to explain. If you lose, you should not be there to explain." 2

Shown below is the Stars and Stripes newspaper's stunning announcement on May 2, 1945:

In the days following Hitler's suicide and the German surrender, there were many Nazi defections and frantic attempts to cover up war crimes. On the other hand, there were others who remained loyal to the Third Reich and continued to fight to the end. If you were called a "Nazi fanatic," it was typically meant as a compliment. It signified you were totally committed to the cause. This was a dangerous period of confusion, lawlessness, and lack of discipline.

D-Day was June 6, 1944. Nearly a year had elapsed since Allied blood was shed on the beaches of Normandy. The war in Europe was finally coming to an end 332 days later.

On the precise day, May 5, that a cease-fire on the southern front was to become effective at noon-time, American troops teamed up with German Wehrmacht soldiers in an improbable battle to defend an Alpine fortress housing French VIP prisoners against Germany's dreaded Waffen-SS.

The *Wehrmacht* ("Defense Force") consisted of the regular German military. It included the *Heer* "Army," the *Kriesmarine* ("Navy,") and the *Luftwaffe* ("Air Force.") The black-uniformed Waffen-SS had swelled to 38 divisions or 900,000 troops by the end of the war. *Waffen* means "Armed" and the SS is an abbreviation for *Schutzstaffel* or "Protective Echelon." These elite warriors were given membership in the Nazi party, and brainwashed to believe they had a life mission to serve the cause of the Third Reich. The recruiting poster on the following page shows the image the Waffen-SS wanted to portray:

Nazi German poster
Courtesy CC0, via Wikimedia Commons

The Waffen-SS fought battles with legendary ferocity. They were well-trained, well-armed, and highly motivated. Most of all, they had a well-earned reputation for brutality. Even in the last days of the war with Hitler dead and Allied victory inevitable, they remained stubbornly loyal to the Nazi regime. They reported directly to Heinrich Himmler and were not accountable to the military. Therefore, they are usually termed a "paramilitary" organization. At the Nuremberg Trials after the war, they were found guilty of numerous war crimes and, in fact, branded as a "criminal organization."

Heinrich Himmler Visiting Dachau
By Bundesarchiv, Bild 152-11-12 / CC BY-SA 3.0 de

Himmler was one of the key henchmen that Hitler used to carry out his nightmarish plans. Others who were significant players include Reichsminister of Propaganda **Hermann Goering**; founder of the Gestapo Joseph Goebbels, who committed suicide along with his wife and children in Hitler's bunker; and Martin Bormann who carried the title of Secretary but functioned as Chief of Staff. It was Grand Admiral Karl Doenitz, though, who was named the Führer's successor. His reign lasted just a week until the Germans signed an unconditional surrender.

Any description of Himmler's depravity would probably be an understatement. Here are some of his own chilling words that give insight into the man:

> "It is the curse of the great to have to walk over corpses." 3

> "The best political weapon is the weapon of terror. Cruelty commands respect. Many may hate us but we don't ask for their love, only for their fear." 4

When Himmler assumed leadership of the SS in 1929, the organization was simply a 300-person personal bodyguard for Adolf Hitler. By 1944, the SS included upwards of a million members and, in addition to the Waffen, controlled organizations such as the Gestapo (Secret Police), the Sicherheitsdienst (Intelligence Service) and Totenkopfverbände (Concentration Camp Guards.)

You might think that an enemy that knows it's losing a war wouldn't be dangerous. You might think it would be demoralized, downtrodden, and disillusioned. Some are like that. They lay down their weapons, surrender at the first opportunity, and are focused only on returning home. They don't want to hurt anyone. They certainly don't want anyone to hurt them.

War correspondent Meyer Levin described this type of scene in the Austrian countryside in early May of 1945:

> "Germans began to leak out of the woods. Some were just boys of sixteen who claimed they hadn't even fired their guns. Then came the older men who all, of course, claimed they had been forced into the fight against their will. There were short bursts of fire – machine guns, burp guns, ours, theirs. The

> tanks reached the village. They let out a long roll of machine-gun fire and presently a few dozen Jerries (Germans) came piling out of the houses, hands up." 5

On the other hand, there are others who are like cornered animals ready to viciously lash out at anyone or anything that gets in their way. These people may resort to reckless, often lawless behavior, feeling they have nothing to lose. They may behave in irrational ways because they're frightened. They often feel resentful that they sacrificed so much for a losing cause. Former French Prime Minister Edouard Daladier wrote about the helpful role that Czechoslovakian cook Andréas Krobot played in keeping the prisoners at Itter Castle informed about the comings and goings of the SS guards:

> "The young Czech who waits on the SS and hears as and sees everything told me that we had to be on our guard. Some of the SS were talking about suicide. Others planned to seize all the food supplies, drink all the beer, and the few bottles of wine that are kept in the cellar, get drunk, and shoot us. The two faces of Germany." 6

The *Schloss* ("Castle" in English) Itter story features both types of people. There were Germans who were disillusioned with the Nazi cause, ready to defect, and actually willing to help the Allies. But, there were also fanatics who were ready to fight to their death. They were capable of committing atrocities to seek revenge, using innocent civilians as targets for their frustration, or simply executing others to try to cover up their crimes.

There was a lot of drinking amongst the German soldiers during those final days of the war. Some drank to try to forget what they had seen. Others drank to try to forget what they had done.

Ch. 2 - The Setting

Believed to have been first built in the 13th Century, Castle Itter is a medieval-looking fortress overlooking a small village of the same name. The village sits to the east of the fortress, some 2,300 feet above sea level. Hovering above it is Hohe Salve, a 6,000-foot mountain in the middle alpine region in the Austrian state of Tyrol.

The Village of Itter (Viewed from the Castle)
Courtesy Steve Morgan/CC by SA 3.0

The town's one narrow street leads up to an ornamental stone gateway surrounded by densely wooded steep slopes, a stream below and mountains all around. Located on a conical hill, the castle seems like the inspiration for a classic fairy tale. In various phases of its existence, it served as a fortress, hotel, and private residence. There had not been a battle on this site since the Middle Ages.

The Countryside around Castle Itter
Courtesy Panoramio

Over the centuries, several structures were built on the site that over time became home to members of royalty as well as the Catholic Church hierarchy. It was even the summer residence of the Pope for many years. In 1812, Napoleon Bonaparte laid claim to the castle as a war prize.

The modern version of the fortress was built in 1878. Four years later, it was bought by German pianist Sophie Menter a student of Franz Liszt who called her his "piano daughter," touting her as the world's best female piano player. She went on to compose music with Pvotr Tchaikovsky at the castle. Sold in 1902, Itter Castle was remodeled in its present Tudor Revival style and used as a hotel. In 1925, it was purchased by Dr. Franz Grüner, the Deputy Governor of the state of Tyrol, who used it to house his large collection of artwork and sculptures. After the Anschluss in 1938, the fortress was leased by the German government.

German Anti-Smoking Poster
Courtesy "Today in History" blog

"Dienftraume" in German means "Dreams of Service." In other words, the poster shown above suggests that quitting smoking is the first step in serving the Third Reich.

When Nazis came to power, they would not tolerate any perceived threat to the health of the Aryan "master race." For the Third Reich, anti-smoking became a crusade. Itter Castle became headquarters for the "German Association for Combating the Dangers of Tobacco," an alliance for promoting the dangers of smoking. Hitler himself quit a two-pack-a-day habit back in 1919. By the start of WWII, der Führer had a standing offer of a gold watch to anyone in his inner circle who quit the habit.

In 1942, Waffen-SS leader Heinrich Himmler set his sights on the fortress and requested that it be repurposed for ominous-sounding "special SS use." On February 7, 1943 Lieutenant General Oswald Pohl, under orders from Himmler, terminated the castle's lease agreement with Dr. Gruner and seized the property with the intent of converting it to a Nazi holding cell. Himmler believed there was a need for temporary housing in Austria of important political prisoners until they could be transported to various German prisons and concentration camps. He was also mindful of the fact that the so-called "honor prisoners" might serve as bargaining chips in the future.

There were 19 VIP rooms constructed - 1 through 5 on the first floor, 6 through 9 on the second, and 10 through 19 on the third. The entire fourth floor was a luxury suite that was given to the commandant.

The transformation of the castle into a prison was completed on April 25, 1943 and the facility was placed under the administration of the Dachau concentration camp, some 145 kilometers away. Castles are fortresses made to prevent entry. The walls are sturdy and thick and there are many vantage points that provide excellent cover. In addition, the moat and large gatehouse made it ideal to be converted into what became regarded as an impenetrable lockup.

The Castle Itter Gatehouse
Courtesy Atlas Obscura

The construction project at Itter was spearheaded by architect Albert Speer, Minister of Armaments and War Production. He used 27 prisoners, both from Dachau and the nearby Flossenbürg camps to act as his labor force. Over the following month, the castle's guest rooms were turned into prison cells.

Itter Castle officially became fully operational as a VIP Prison on April 25, 1943. It served as one of nearly 200 sub-camps and satellite facilities across Southern Germany and Northern Austria that were part of the Dachau Concentration Camp.

Castle Itter in Winter
Courtesy History Collection

The prison was established to contain prisoners who could prove valuable to the Reich, including former French Prime Ministers Édouard Daladier and Paul Reynaud, retired Commanders of the French Army Generals Maxime Weygand and Maurice Gamelin, Leader of the Free French Charles de Gaulle's elder sister Marie-Agnès Cailliau, right-wing fascist leader François de La Rocque, the former head of France's largest trade union Léon Jouhaux, and anti-Fascist Michel Clemenceau whose father Georges served twice as Prime Minister of France. The prisoners even included a tennis player – Jean Borotra. He was no ordinary player. At one time, he was ranked #1 in the world. The castle also held a number of detainees from Dachau, who were used for maintenance and other menial work.

War correspondent Meyer Levin called the imprisoned dignitaries "The biggest bag of the biggest big shots." 7 They were known as being in "ehrenhäftlinge" in German which means "special or honor detention."

Marie-Agnes (de Gaulle) Cailliau responded to the call of her younger brother Charles by joining the French Resistance. She and her husband were arrested in 1943 and held for fourteen months in Fresnes prison, then deported to Bad Godesberg, an annex of the Buchenwald concentration camp. The Caillliau couple was transferred to Castle Itter in April of 1945. Marie-Agnes tried to convince the honor prisoners to put concern for France above their own political preferences. She tried to no avail to have them get along with each other to present a united front to the Germans.

Marie –Agnes Cailliau
Courtesy of the Bibliothèque Nationale, Paris

Paul Reynaud
Courtesy of the Bibliothèque Nationale, Paris

Edouard Daladier
Courtesy of the Bibliothèque Nationale, Paris

The captives were a diverse group politically and, in fact, some were bitter enemies. Former Prime Ministers Daladier and Reynaud were rivals who disliked each other as much as they both hated General Weygand. The latter served honorably in World War I and was, in fact, the one who delivered the terms of the armistice that ended that conflict.

General Maxime Weygand
Courtesy of the Bibliothèque Nationale, Paris

When the German Wehrmacht began overrunning France in June 1940, however, Weygand not only pushed for an armistice but openly collaborated with the Germans as part of the Fascist Vichy French Government. General Gamelin, was equally resentful of Weygand who succeeded him as Commander of the Army during the Battle of France. There were also tensions between conservative leader de La Rocque and the liberal Unionist Jouhaux. The prisoners segregated themselves based on their political views, and were often more at odds with each other than they were with their captors.

The average age of the VIP's group was 65. The youngest, at 35, was Paul Reynaud's secretary and mistress, Christiane Mabire who brought a typewriter which she used to help him write his memoirs.

General Maurice Gamelin
Courtesy of the Bibliothèque Nationale, Paris

Francois de La Rocque
Courtesy of the Bibliothèque Nationale, Paris

Leon Jouhaux
Courtesy of the Bibliothèque Nationale, Paris

Michel Clemenceau
Courtesy of the Bibliothèque Nationale, Paris

The eldest honor prisoner, in his late 70's was General Weygand. For his role in the surrender of France in 1940 and his involvement in the Vichy government, Weygand was reviled by many of his countrymen. At Castle Itter, Reynaud took on the role of spokesperson for those who felt betrayed by the government. Reynaud refused to shake hands with or even talk to Weygand. Instead, he took every opportunity, when the general was in hearing range, to refer to him as a traitor and Nazi collaborator.

Some 800 years after the original version was built, Castle Itter would become the sight of one of the strangest battles ever fought. According to war correspondent Meyer Levin, the story of the battle is "an adventure all trimmed up with secret emissaries, trick escapes, traitors, cut wires, a beleaguered castle, and fanatic SS men." [7]

There are several heroes that played a vital role in this true tale. They seem like characters right out of central casting. First, there was the hard-drinking, cigar-smoking, tough guy American Army Captain named Jack Lee. It's hard to imagine a more American-sounding name. There was Major Josef Gangl, a German officer with a conscience, who was increasingly troubled by the Nazi atrocities until he finally decided to switch sides and join the Austrian resistance, even providing them with Wehrmacht weapons. He knew, of course, that this act of treason would be punishable by death but was willing to take the risk.

Then, there was the straight-edge Captain Kurt Siegfried Schrader who quit the Waffen-SS and, concluding that the war was hopelessly lost and it made no sense to incur additional casualties, subsequently agreed to take charge of the castle defense against his former organization. Finally, there was Borotra, the flamboyant showman of a tennis player, who volunteered for what seemed to be a suicide mission in a desperate effort to seek help during the battle.

The SS gave command of the prison to Captain Sebastian Wimmer, a former police officer from Munich who had a reputation for brutality and cruelty. The ordinary prisoners lost their individual identities once their prison numbers were tattooed on their arms. The honor prisoners were always referred to by name. It's as if they were important enough to be allowed to keep their identities. Former Prime Minister Edouard Daladier drew a contrast between the way Wimmer treated the two groups:

> "The camp commandant, SS Captain Sebastian Wimmer was, by nature, a brutish and cruel man. He had tortured prisoners at Dachau with no visible remorse and was given to drunken bouts of ranting and raging when given bad news. He was a tyrant with respect to the 'numbered prisoners' but treated the French honor prisoners with grudging respect and courtesy, something expected of him by the Gestapo. It was his hope
> that after the war the French would speak positively of him, since all officers in the SS were considered de

facto war criminals whenever they were captured by the Allies. Wimmer's family was stationed with him at Castle Itter, which added to his anxiety; he was anxious to keep them alive." 8

A native Bavarian, Wimmer was born in Dingolfin. He joined the Munich police department as a patrolman and rose to the rank of sergeant. He had a reputation for securing quick confessions by savagely beating suspects during interrogations. Recruited by the SS, he took part in several campaigns across Europe with the elite Panzer Divisions and was involved in some of the most horrific acts committed by the Nazi regime during the war. Wimmer's ruthless behavior helped him rise through the ranks of the SS. He was put in charge of the Majdanek concentration camp near Lublin, Poland prior to being assigned to Castle Itter.

Emblem of SS-Totenkopfverbände
Courtesy Blogspot

Under his command at the castle were two-dozen soldiers from the dreaded *SS-Totenkopfverbände* or "Death's-head Units," who were responsible for running the concentration camps in Europe during World War II. Wimmer was a notoriously sadistic and volatile sociopath. He was also known to be someone who got results so the combination of traits made him a rising Nazi star. He held escape drills and surprise inspections to whip the guard force into shape.

The first three VIP's to arrive were former Prime Minister Édouard Daladier, General Maurice Gamelin, and Trade Union leader Léon Jouhaux. Daladier was actually familiar with the castle, having spent time at Schloss Itter in 1935 as a guest of Dr. Grüner.

Wimmer addressed the camp guards immediately after the arrival of Daladier, Gamelin, and Jouhaux. He wanted to be certain that they understood that these VIP's were not to be treated like other inmates of Dachau:

> "The three people who have just arrived to be imprisoned in the castle are French. They will be joined by others. By command of the Führer, these prisoners are to be viewed as hostages. Upon meeting one of them you should salute them with a regular military salute, and not with the Führer salute. If one of these gentlemen should attempt to speak to you, your response should be the following: 'Your Excellency, would you please speak to Commandant Wimmer?'" 9

The French honor prisoners were certainly given special treatment. They slept in converted guest rooms, were served full-course meals, were given free access to the castle library, and were even allowed to exercise in the courtyard area. The guards were more like servants. The Nazi government considered the honor prisoners as potential assets that were valuable enough to be kept alive for political leverage. The living conditions at the castle could not have been a sharper contrast to the living (or more accurately the dying) conditions endured by the numbered prisoners.

The VIP's could choose to eat their three meals each day in the dining room, out on the open-air terrace, or as take-out to eat in their rooms. Each received a monthly allowance of 100 liters of wine as well as 500 Reichsmarks with which they could buy items from a small store on the castle grounds.

Imagine the horrific scene if you juxtaposed images of the numbered prisoners being starved, tortured, and gassed at other Dachau locations while those who were too important to be numbered would be served their meals as if they were at a restaurant. You can't help but wonder how concerned the VIP's were about the inhumane treatment given to the numbered prisoners being held at the death camps.

Located ten miles northwest of Munich, Dachau, one of the Nazi's first concentration camps was opened in March, 1933. With the increasing persecution of "undesirables," Dachau's inmate population soared. During the war, the camp became an important source of slave labor, especially for the military industries. Thirty-seven subsidiary locations were built to house armaments workers. Shown on the next page is the infamous front gate at Dachau with the ironic sign, found at many concentration camps which says, "Work Sets You Free" in English.

Courtesy Trip Advisor

Toward the end of the war, Dachau received large numbers of inmates from other camps the Germans were forced to abandon as they retreated. Plans were drawn up for the killing of all prisoners, but before the act could be carried out, elements of the American 7th Army began to free those in the Dachau camps. The main location was liberated on April 29, 1945.

Combat Medic Bernard Rice said this about the horrors he saw first-hand at Dachau:

> "Up close we saw that they were emaciated; their bodies were just skin over bone. They spoke in high-pitched, almost birdlike voices. They carried nothing. They could hardly put one foot ahead of the

other. Their only clothing was thin, striped rags although the air was cold…This was our first encounter with the German concentration camps. The people we met were inmates who had escaped from a satellite of the Dachau camp as the Germans retreated. We were not prepared for this. We had seen death almost daily during the previous five months, but the dead up to now were mostly one or two at a time. Even our bloodiest battle could not prepare us for Dachau. There we found hundreds of dead. Some lay in grotesque piles, some neatly stacked like cordwood, others thrown helter-skelter into a pit. This was Hitler's 'Final Solution,' eliminate all of Europe's Jews and anyone else who opposed Hitler. Words cannot describe what we saw nor the feelings of revulsion we felt." 10

Ch. 3 - The Handyman

Former Prime Minister Edouard Daladier noticed a change in the attitude of the Germans as the Allies were closing in on Berlin claiming, "I could see dejection on the faces of the sentinels and consternation in the eyes of the soldiers as they busily went about their chores, as they do every day." 11

The VIP prisoners expressed their increasing concern to Commandant Sebastian Wimmer that the Waffen-SS could soon attack Itter Castle. They felt that Himmler might give an official order to assassinate the prisoners or rogue troops might simply act on their own. He assured them that he would take responsibility to see that no harm came to them.

Rather than simply taking Wimmer's word for it, the prisoners asked Zvonimir Čučković to help them. A member of the Yugoslav Communist Resistance, Čučković fought against the Nazis before he was captured. A veteran of the Dachau concentration camp, he worked as an electrician and handyman at the castle and helped convert it to a prison during the construction phase. Zvonimir was a 36-year-old Croatian who had made his living as an electrician before the German invasion of April of 1941. After the attack, he joined the National Liberation Army, a Yugoslav resistance group, and was arrested by the Gestapo in December of 1941. He spent time in several Nazi prison camps before ending up in Dachau in September of 1942. His proficiency as an electrician likely saved him from being executed.

Now, years later, he had earned prison Commandant Sebastian Wimmer's trust and was allowed occasional access to/from the castle, despite being a numbered prisoner. Before he left, the French honor prisoners asked for Čučković's help in conducting a daring mission. He readily agreed.

The first step was to find a plausible reason for Zvonimir, nicknamed Zvonko, to leave the castle. It came that very day. Just before noon on May 3, Čučković was working in the garage when the Commandant walked in and asked, "Do you have enough parts to finish installing the electric bedside lamps in the farmhouse?"

At that point, Wimmer was very anxious to move his family to a new residence in a nearby town, hoping to avoid the advancing Allied troops by blending into the civilian population.

Čučković replied, "Sir, I have enough material."

"Good, you will accompany Sergeant Euba on foot this afternoon and ensure that there is electricity in those two lamps," instructed Wimmer.

Knowing that traveling with one of the castle's guards would prevent, or at least greatly complicate, his escape, Zvonko replied that he could accomplish his task more efficiently if he were allowed to go by himself on a bicycle. Wimmer turned and walked away. Worrying that he might have somehow given himself away, Čučković stood there, trying to decide what to do next.

Wimmer returned with a bicycle saying, "I've put your tools in the basket."

Čučković pushed the bike to the front gate, which Wimmer unlocked and pulled open. Wimmer said, "Be quick about it."

Čučković replied "I will be, Captain," and began pedaling up the Schlossweg, the access road leading to Itter village. As he passed St. Joseph's Church, the Catholic handyman said a quick prayer: "Dear Lord, please help me get to the Americans today." 12

Rather than heading to Wimmer's new home, he made his way through German lines to the American forces in Innsbruck. He was carrying a letter in his pocket written in English by Paul Reynaud's secretary and mistress, Christiane Mabire, detailing their situation and giving their location. Seeking Allied assistance, he was to give the letter to the first American soldiers he encountered.

He rode his bicycle 8 kilometers to the town of Wörgl, where Waffen-SS troops were going door-to-door rounding up suspected deserters. Čučković chose to press on up the Inn

River valley towards Innsbrook, a distance of 64 km. About 6½ kilometers along the way, though, he was ordered to halt by a squad of troops from the Grossdeutschland Wehrmacht Division at a road junction.

An officer began walking to Čučković with his automatic pistol drawn and pointed at his head. "Who are you and where are you going?" he demanded.

"Sir, I am on the way to Kundl," replied Čučković in his most deferential voice.

"What do you want there?" challenged the German.

Thinking quickly, Zvonimir said, "Sir, Captain Wimmer at Schloss Itter ordered me to install some electric lights. He told me it was very important that I do the work and return quickly."

Noticing the tools in the bicycle basket, the officer's demeanor suddenly changed to indifference as he said, "On your way, then" and waved Zvonko on. Letting out a sigh of relief, the Croat knew the letter he carried in his pocket asking for help from the Americans would condemn him to an immediate death if the German officer had been suspicious enough to search him.

A few more kilometers down the road, a Waffen-SS officer stopped Čučković and was also convinced enough by his story to let him pass. Shortly after the second encounter, Zvonimir stopped to rest and noticed a military vehicle coming toward him. It sped past and then stopped to pick up a soldier on a bridge. Seconds after the truck moved on, a huge explosion demolished the overpass. A startled Čučković jumped back on his bicycle and began pedaling quickly down the road. Trying to spur himself on, he muttered, "Forward, Zvonko, you're in no man's land!" 13

He reached the outskirts of the city late that evening and encountered elements of the 409th Regiment of the American 103rd Infantry Division of the US VI Corps at the outskirts of Innsbruck. He gave the officer in charge, Major John T. Kramers, the letter which read:

> "The American military authorities are hereby informed that the undernamed French statesmen, generals, ladies and personalities are confined in the castle of Itter. The village and castle of Itter is eight kilometers east of Wörgl."

The note listed the names of the prisoners and also contained a strange sentence sounding like something from a travel agent - "They have plenty of trunks and bags."

Did the Americans believe what Zvonimir Čučković had to say? "Of course," answered Levin. "His name sounded too improbable to have been invented." 14

Major Kramers asked Zvonimir, "How did you manage to get out of the place?"

"Why, the Commander sent me out," he responded. Obviously, that wasn't quite true. Sebastian Wimmer was completely unaware of Zvonimir's mission. Despite being a frequent victim of Wimmer's drunken outbursts, Zvonko would always be grateful to him for saving his life by choosing to remove him from Dachau Concentration Camp because of his skill as an electrician to have him work at the castle. So, it was a small matter to overlook having been bullied and put in a good word for Wimmer.

Major John Kramers
Courtesy warhistoryonline.com

Wimmer was very careful not to mistreat the honor prisoners under his watch. The numbered prisoners, including both Čučković and Krobot were a different story. Several incidents took place in the months preceding the battle of Castle Itter, when tensions were rising as the Allies closed in on Berlin and Wimmer increased his drinking.

In one instance, Zvonimir was in the garage, working on trying to fix the windshield wiper on Wimmer's car. Unnoticed, Wimmer entered, clenched his fist, and punched Čučković in the face. Zvonko, knowing that he should not defend himself or even utter a word, simply stood there. **Wimmer hit him again and was about to punch him a third time when he realized that General Gamelin had** witnessed this incident. The general was out on his daily constitutional and happened to be passing by. He reprimanded the commandant saying, "You are not allowed to hit a prisoner." Wimmer left and was not seen for two days after the incident.

Another time, Wimmer called Čučković to the guardhouse and started berating him for not fixing a leaky toilet in the Commandant's suite. Zvonimir indicated that he had ordered a replacement rubber washer from the supply depot but it hadn't yet arrived. Wimmer shouted that he wasn't interested in excuses.

There had been a heavy snowfall that day. He ordered the Croat to spend the next two nights, from 6 p.m. to 6 a.m., shoveling snow in the courtyard. Two guards were told to watch him to make sure that he didn't shirk on his responsibility. They not only supervised but, unknown to Wimmer, actually helped the exhausted Zvonimir. 15

Kramers continued the questioning by asking, "What Commander? The German Commander?"

"Yes, the German Commander," explained Zoonimir. "You see, he is responsible for the safety of these important people, and he is afraid the SS might shoot his prisoners at the last minute. So, he hoped the Americans will come quickly."

Major Kramers showed the note to the division's French Liaison Officer, Lt. Eric Lutten, who recognized the names of the eclectic group that represented the extremes of French politics.

Lutten remarked:

> "To lock up in one castle a group such as this! A Labor Leader and a Fascist Leader, two Prime Ministers and the Generals who had failed them, a Vichy cabinet member, and the sister of the leader of the French Resistance. But certainly these French personalities had to be rescued –
> some of them because they deserved freedom, others because the state would want an explanation of their conduct. Yes, the castle of Itter contained a hatful." 16

Kramers informed headquarters of the situation and soon received permission to conduct a rescue mission with a heavily-armed task force consisting of four tank destroyers, several jeeps, a truckload of soldiers and, yes, a large empty truck for the trunks and baggage of the VIP prisoners. Kramers and Lutten pored over a map of northern Tyrol and plotted out a route that would take them to the castle via the same path Čučković had taken on his bicycle.

Departing at dawn the next morning, May 5, the rescue force encountered cheering Polish, Czech, French and Russian ex-prisoners on the road to Wörgl. The convey was stopped at a crossroad about 32 kilometers out by some Austrian partisans. They described an altercation they had had with the SS further up the road who were acting as rear guard for vehicles heading for the mountains. Kramers decided to press on.

They began encountering heavy shelling just past Jenbach, around halfway to Itter. Levin reported:

> "Our little party paused for reflection. There we were, alone in what was still Krautland. Liberating a castleful of big names was sure important, but it was also important not to get killed in so doing, especially on the day when fighting was supposed to have stopped. To add point to the argument, there came a familiar whine, which we thought we had heard for the last time." 17

The whine was followed by a blast from a German 88-mm anti-aircraft and anti-tank artillery gun. The 88 was arguably the most valuable artillery piece used by any army during the war. It was feared by Allied airmen, tankers, and foot soldiers because of its deadly accuracy and versatility.

88 mm Flak 37
Courtesy Guns America

The American tanks pulled off the road and parked under some trees for cover. The soldiers jumped from their trucks, took positions in a ditch, and watched the shells come down.

One of them said, "They've seen us."

Another offered, "If they're shooting at us, that's lousy poor shooting."

"Yeah, but it's eighty-eights and they got observation on this road," claimed the first soldier.

Major Kramers did a quick reconnaissance and reported the situation to headquarters who told him to halt the operation immediately. They said that not only would it be too dangerous to proceed to Itter but, if they went further, they would be encroaching into what was now territory of the 36th Infantry Division. Kramers was understandably angry and wasn't going to let a little thing like a direct order stop him.

Meanwhile back at the castle, some shocking events had just taken place that no one could have anticipated.

Ch. 4 - The Suicide and the Escape

Former Prime Minister Edouard Daladier kept a radio in his room that was smuggled in for him by Zvonimir Čučković. He would listen to BBC broadcasts and keep the others informed as to the progress of the war. The other ex-Prime Minister, Paul Reynaud, recalled:

> "Every morning we used to listen to the BBC. It was with great excitement that we learned of the collapse of Mussolini, of the triumphs in Italy, and with even more enthusiasm, of the landing in Normandy, the liberation of Paris, and the success of the Allied Armies." 18

The VIP prisoners were convinced, however, that with the impending collapse of Nazi Germany, the SS would begin exterminating prisoners to try to cover up their crimes.

In April, Daladier and Reynaud had met with Captain Sebastian Wimmer to discuss their fate. With Michel Clemenceau acting as a translator, the French warned Wimmer that since he was the commandant of the prison, if anything were to happen to the POW's, he would be held responsible.

Reynaud said that Clemenceau confronted Wimmer directly:

"It is possible that before too long you may get an order to hand over the prisoners. You well know what it will be for. You must know what the Allied authorities would think of such an action. What are your intentions? 19

Captain Wimmer assured him, "I would do whatever I could to help you and the other prisoners survive, and if possible, escape." Wimmer would soon go on to break his promise.

On April 29, U.S. troops captured the main camp at Dachau, liberating its long-suffering captives. Soon, all the satellite camps across Southern Germany would be freed. The extent of the holocaust was being revealed to the world.

The honor prisoners at Itter had witnessed a steady stream of high-ranking SS officers and other war criminals stopping there to requisition fuel and supplies before heading into the mountains. The castle was suddenly visited by the Commandant of the Dachau Concentration Camp, SS Lieutenant-Colonel Wilhelm Eduard Weiter on April 30. His official title was more than a mouthful - *Schutzstaffel Obersturmbannführer*.

Weiter was born the son of a saddlery shop owner. His father sold horse saddles, whips, and harnesses. Upon graduation from high school, he became a book salesman. Then, at 20 years old, he joined the army for 10 years, finishing as a Regimental Paymaster. After his discharge, with the rank of major, he joined the Bavarian Police Force, also as a paymaster. He joined the Waffen-SS and, again, was a paymaster until becoming an administration officer at Dachau. On September 30, 1943, he was appointed to replace Martin Weiss as the eighth Commandant at Dachau.

Wilhelm was not the typical SS Officer. He was described as "wanting to sit out the war behind a desk" and "a half-hearted Nazi." He rarely got involved with the inmates, preferring to delegate the day-to-day running of the concentration camp to his subordinates. Consequently, conditions deteriorated and Dachau suffered from overcrowding. Weiter did little to expand the camp to keep up with the influx of inmates.

It has been speculated that Heinrich Himmler had issued an order, codenamed "Volkenbrand," to murder all the inmates to prevent them falling into Allied hands but Weiter refused to comply. If this is true, it certainly explains why Wilhelm suddenly abandoned his post at Dachau and wanted to "disappear."

Unofficially, he was known as "The Butcher of Dachau" but there is little evidence to suggest he was much more than a bureaucrat who let others do the dirty work. Former Prime Minister Edouard Daladier described the 56-year-old Weiter as "obese and apoplectic, with the face of a brute."

At dinner that night, Weiter drunkenly bragged to Castle Commandant Wimmer about the way the prisoners were abused at Dachau. He also boasted that he had ordered the death of two thousand prisoners the day before leaving the camp. The more he drank, the louder and more obnoxious he got.

Wimmer gave him what was considered the best guest room, next door to Renaud. On the morning of May 2, two gunshots rang out inside the castle. The guards and prisoners awoke to a gruesome discovery. Eduard Weiter died of apparent suicide.

The chief executioner of Dachau had committed his last execution. It happened to be his own. His first shot in the chest had failed. The second shot went through his head. It may be that he felt remorse for the atrocities he had committed. His gloating the night before may have been a sort of confession of guilt. It was also likely that he simply wanted to avoid being captured and put on trial for the war crimes he had committed. Both reasons may have been factors.

Weiter's SS entourage tried to bury him in a little cemetery just outside the Itter castle bridge, but the brave village priest, Father Höck, refused to have him interred on what he considered to be consecrated ground. They wound up dragging Weiter out of the castle feet first, wrapping him in a sheet and digging a grave for him on the hillside. Hearing that Americans were on the road, the Nazis quickly left the castle to escape further into the Alps.

It was two days later, in the early morning hours of May 4, that Wimmer and his men abandoned Castle Itter. German resistance was continuing to collapse, and with his superiors dead, captured, or on the run, Wimmer felt there was little reason to stay. When Čučković failed to return and with the death of Weiter, Wimmer was frightened. He abandoned entirely the idea of hiding out in his new home.

He had received a call informing him that American rescuers were on their way to the castle. He bid his charges farewell, piled his wife and belongings into a car and departed. It was an unlikely prison escape because it was not made by the prisoners. It was made by the person in charge of the prison.

Wimmer gathered the VIP's together announcing, "I intend to evacuate the castle today with my SS force and hope you will provide testimonial as to my fair treatment of you."

There was debate before the VIP's concluded that they grant Wimmer his request. Chief among the dissenters was Paul Reynaud:

> "My own view was that we should not do so since we would not be safe until the castle was occupied by the Americans. However, we did give it to him but not until we had gained possession of some arms. For myself, I took a tommy-gun and some ammunition." [20]

Soon after, the rest of the guards left and the VIP's found themselves in control of Castle Itter. They proceeded to the armory, seizing whatever small weapons had been left behind. They agreed that it would be too dangerous to leave the castle since they could be easily recognized. The consensus was that they should wait and hope for the Allies to arrive. On the other hand, with German forces still roaming the area, the former prisoners were determined to continue their efforts to try to reach out to nearby Allies.

That same day, May 4, the "Red-White-Red" (a radio station for Austrian partisans) in Innsbruck issued the following appeal, repeated several times: "Attention. The former French government is interned at Schloss Itter. The population is asked to take care of the imprisoned!"

The well-intentioned message alerted the Allies and the Resistance of the existence and exact location of the VIP prisoners. There was only one problem. It may also have alerted the Nazis.

Ch. 5 - The Waffen-SS Captain

Before he abandoned the castle, Sebastian Wimmer contacted a personal friend, 29-year-old Kurt Siegfried Schrader. A Waffen-SS captain, Schrader had recently returned home to the village of Itter and was now wearing civilian clothes having been "discharged" from the army. Wimmer, to his credit, remembered his pledge to the VIP prisoners and asked Kurt to look after the safety of those being held in the castle. The captain agreed.

Captain Kurt Siegfried Schrader
Courtesy real-life-heroes.fandom.com/wiki/File:Kurt_Siegfried_Schrader

Schrader had gradually grown disillusioned with the German war effort. A decorated combat veteran from Magdeburg, Germany, he had served in several campaigns across Europe during World War II and suffered serious injuries during both the Siege of Leningrad and the Battle of Normandy.

In January 1945, he was transferred to a military hospital in Wörgl, Austria. He brought his wife and two daughters to the village of Itter so they could live together in relative safety from the Allied bombing of Germany. During this time, he made regular visits to his friend, Captain Sebastian Wimmer at Castle Itter. Kurt also frequently fraternized with the POW's being held there. He was even willing to take the risk of letting them know of his growing anti-Nazi sentiments.

Early in 1945, Captain Schrader was recalled to active duty. He was not in physical condition for combat and required two canes to walk, but Germany was suffering a serious shortage in manpower and anyone who could fire a weapon was put on the front lines.

Schrader took part in the defense of the Ludendorff Bridge at Remagen, Germany. Despite fierce resistance, U.S. troops succeeded in capturing the bridge on March 7. After barely escaping from Remagen, he was sent east to defend Budapest, Hungary from the advancing Russians. By the time he reached Vienna, though, Budapest had already fallen. Kurt decided to make his way west, but during his journey, British fighter aircraft attacked and destroyed the locomotive of his train. Schrader was careful to point out that this was a civilian and not a military train. The implication is that there were atrocities committed by both sides in the war. In an unpublished personal memoir, Schrader described the unfortunate event this way:

> "The planes returned again and again shooting at us, like in a rabbit hunt. After several hours we were finally able to continue the journey with a replacement locomotive; in the evening I arrived at Itter and was reconciled with my family." 21

Schrader was next put in charge of German logistical operations for Lieutenant Colonel Johann Giel's battle group. While stationed there, he shared his feelings with a number of Wehrmacht officers who believed, too, that the war was lost. Such opinions were extremely dangerous as the SS and Gestapo brutally executed any Germans who expressed anti-war or anti-Nazi sentiments. Despite the risks, Schrader and his colleagues approached Colonel Giehl, and convinced him that further resistance was pointless and continued fighting would only needlessly waste the lives of more German soldiers. After their meeting, Giehl issued orders to all troops under his command to cease fighting and surrender to the nearest Allied units.

According to Schrader:

> "Lieutenant Colonel Giehl had become combat group commander as Hitler hoped for another turn of the tide of the war. The military situation, though, changed hourly to our disadvantage and in order to avoid further human casualties, we officers urged Giehl to give up the fight. He, too, accepted the senseless resistance and agreed to our proposal. He asked me to take his wife and children with him to

my family in Itter, because he feared fighting in the Inn Valley near Wörgl." 22

On parting, Giehl handed Schrader a note that he hoped would provide protection if he were stopped and questioned. It read:

"Kampfgruppe Giehl, Kpf.Gr.Gef.Stand, 6 May 1945

Confirmation. SS-Hstuf Schrader, placed himself at my disposal on April 28, 1945 to the service in my staff. Hstuf Schrader, who due to his wound is no longer suitable for an active combat role, was released by me on May 2, 1945 from my staff to his hometown of Itter.

In the absence of an official seal, dated Giehl, Lieutenant Colonel and Commander"

Schrader continued:

"SS-Hauptsturmführer Wimmer from Schloss Itter called me on my last day of duty. He told me that he wanted to leave his post because of the approach of the Americans, and 'disappear' somehow. Shortly before, I had heard from him that he had earlier worked in a concentration camp in Poland. That's all I learned from him but I suspect he carried a guilt complex with him. When I arrived home in the evening, I learned that Wimmer had left the castle with some guards. For me, I assumed, the war was over, and I took off my uniform with more joy than tears." 23

Schrader added:

"Shortly after the special report on the radio, Mme. Brüchlin and Léon Jouhaux came to see me in my apartment; they had also heard the report, as had all the detainees, and asked me, but as quickly as possible, to come to the castle, which was about 200 meters away from my apartment. The French, who knew me, wanted to talk with me. I went there immediately and found almost all the French gathered in the courtyard of the castle. Michel Clemenceau was the spokesman and spoke to me in German and asked me as a German officer to take care of the security of the French internees until the arrival of the Americans. Since there were only a few guards left, I pointed out that it could be very difficult to defend against attacks by retreating German troops." 24

Clemenceau pressed him reasoning, "We would feel more secure if you stayed. In addition, if necessary, you could act as a negotiator in the event of an attack."

The honor prisoners also decided to fly a French tricolor flag from one of the high castle windows to prevent an Allied air attack. This was another move that could prove costly. If a roving Waffen-SS happened to see the flag it could signal that there were targets inside.

Schrader agreed for the second time to help take care of the VIP prisoners. He didn't mention to them that he had already made the same promise to Wimmer. It's not difficult to follow his logic. Kurt was most concerned about himself and his family. You might think he was caught in the middle between the Allies and the Nazis. Someone less clever would have been. But Schrader was able to play both sides. Doing a favor for Wimmer really did nothing for Schrader personally. Wimmer already told him he "would try to disappear" into the mountains, on a boat to South America, or somewhere else.

Schrader had the note from Lieutenant Colonel Giehl that could provide protection if he were detained by the Waffen-SS. Letting the French dignitaries "persuade" him to head the castle defenders would undoubtedly make them beholden to him. Knowing the future would in all likelihood bring a war crimes trial, it would certainly help his cause if the best-known and most important French VIP prisoners would testify that they came to him asking to be protected and that, after negotiating with them, he graciously consented. Assuming all went well, he could later ask them to put something in writing that he could use in case he were put on trial as a member of the Waffen-SS. That would turn out to precisely be the case.

Unlike Wimmer and many of the other Nazis, therefore, Captain Schrader did not feel the need to disappear anywhere. He was confident that he was prepared for whatever might happen. Fearing, however, for his family's safety, he asked for and was given permission to bring his wife and two daughters to the castle. Schrader was, above all, a practical man. He knew how to play the cards he was dealt.

Ch. 6 - The Cook & the Wehrmacht Major

Back at Castle Itter, the VIP's didn't wait long to send out another runner to seek help from the Americans. Even though only a day had passed, they recognized there was a high likelihood that Čuković had been, or would be, killed or captured. Stepping forward to volunteer on May 4 was friend to the prisoners and cook Andréas Krobot, known to the prisoners as André.

Clemenceau and Reynaud felt safe enough that afternoon to take a short walk to Itter village. According to Reynaud:

> "The Austrian flag, white and red, was everywhere. We went along the road down which Wehrmacht troops were pouring westward. We obtained a bicycle from the village shopkeeper and send our faithful friend, the Czech cook André, to Wörgl where he would try to get in touch with the American army. There were no Americans in Wögl, though. A man told André that the Wehrmacht wanted to stop fighting under the terms of the agreement in Italy reached by General Sir Alexander and the commander of the German troops in Italy and Austria but that the S.S. was fighting on." 25

Krobot, like Zvonko, was often a victim of Wimmer's bullying. On March 20, 1945, for example, Zvonko was working on the Commandant's staff car when one of the female numbered prisoners, ran up to him saying Wimmer was about to shoot Andreas

Krobot. Rushing to the kitchen, Čučković found Wimmer pointing his Walther P-38 pistol out an open window at the Czech cook, who was standing in the vegetable garden outside. The terrified women working in the kitchen were standing and sobbing loudly, as Wimmer yelled at Krobot, "You dog, come one step forward and one to the left." Evidently, he was trying to line up a clearer shot. Čučković took a large knife from a nearby rack. He was ready to kill the Commandant if he shot Krobot. Fortunately, that wasn't necessary as Wimmer's wife happened to come around and stop her husband from committing murder. 26

Krobot rode his borrowed bicycle to Wörgl hoping to reach help there. Armed with a note similar to Čučković's, he hoped to contact the Austrian Resistance in the town, which had recently been abandoned by Wehrmacht forces but, unfortunately, reoccupied by roving SS.

In Wörgl, Krobot witnessed Waffen-SS troopers firing into houses that were displaying white flags of surrender or Austrian flags as a symbol of independence. The situation in Wörgl was growing increasingly dangerous, as the Waffen-SS was ruthlessly suppressing potential dissent among the population. Seeking haven from the German shock troops, Krobot just happened to run into a member of the Resistance After the Anschluss, a number of Austrians became part of an underground movement. While they were a small minority, there was an increasingly organized group in Austria fighting against the Nazis. At first the Underground focused mostly on non-violent political forms of resistance, lacking the resources and support for an armed insurgency. Major defeats suffered by Nazi Germany along with a renewed sense of Austrian

Nationalism helped galvanize the movement. In the final days of the war, partisan activity in Austria increased dramatically. Andréas stumbled upon an organized cell of the Resistance operating in Wörgl. The Czech was taken into their care, and then was introduced to a key ally of the Underground, a highly decorated 34-year-old German Wehrmacht officer named Major Josef Gangl.

Gangl had taken the opportunity of the breakdown in command to abandon the German army but, unlike many who had followed that course, he did not desert. Rather, he shifted sides, leading some soldiers to fight for their German homeland in attacks against the Nazi loyalists.

Major Gangl was willing to take on the task of fighting to free the castle prisoners, but was unwilling to sacrifice the few troops he had in what presumably would be a suicidal attack on a heavily defended fortress manned by the SS. Of course, he did not know at the time that the prisoners had been abandoned and were now in charge of the castle. Instead, he was intent on conserving his troops to protect local residents from SS attacks. He was going to pin his hopes on the Americans for help.

Josef "Sepp" Gangl was born in Obertraubling, Bavaria. The son of a Royal Bavarian State Railways official, he joined the Wehrmacht when he was 18 years old and enjoyed a distinguished career, primarily as an artillery officer. Gangl began World War II as an *Oberfeldwebel* (the equivalent of a Sergeant First Class.) He was wounded in the opening salvoes of the war and spent six months recuperating in hospitals. In May of 1940, he returned to service as commander of a reconnaissance unit in the Wehrmacht's 25th Infantry Division.

Major Josef Gangl
Courtesy Julieu Jääseläiner,/CC BY 2.0

Gangl fought in the Battle of France and the Battle of Normandy. After the Battle of the Bulge, his unit was sent south to help defend the German town of Saarbrücken near the French border. Gangl and his men put up determined resistance but their efforts were futile, as German defenses were overwhelmed by units of the U.S. Seventh Army. After the battle, Sepp was promoted to major and given command of the 2nd Battalion of Volks-Werfer Brigade 7. His unit was barely at half strength, with a limited number of vehicles and a few artillery pieces. At this point in the war, there was almost no hope of reinforcement or re-supply. Beleaguered German forces were relentlessly pushed back as the Allies advanced across Germany in overwhelming force.

By April 1945, Volks-Werfer Brigade 7 was no longer an effective fighting force, and Sepp's battalion was badly decimated. The Brigadier General ordered all remaining units to break up and head for Austria to join defenses being set up across the Alps. When Major Gangl entered Austria, he only had thirty soldiers left from his entire Battalion. They ended up in Wörgl, joining the battle group led by Lieutenant Colonel Giehl. Soon he made contact with members of the local Austria Resistance and agreed to help provide them with weapons, supplies, and intelligence.

Gangl had become disillusioned with the war effort. He had no intention of having any more of his men die for the Nazi cause. Sepp took an extraordinary risk helping the Austrians since it not only endangered him but also put his wife and two children at risk of reprisals by the Gestapo and SS. He quickly earned the trust of members of the Underground, and on April 30, leaders of the Austrian Resistance had placed Gangl in charge of military operations in the Wörgl sector.

Major Gangl was informed by the Resistance about the prison at Castle Itter and began planning for a German-Austrian raid to rescue the POW's. The heavy presence of Waffen-SS troops in the area made such an operation very risky as he sought to avoid a battle with superior forces. The sudden appearance of Andréas Krobot on May 4, with news of the situation at Castle Itter changed those plans.

The major was caught in a dire predicament. He wanted to rescue the French dignitaries, but he also wanted to keep the soldiers under his command alive. He also had pledged to help the Resistance protect the citizens of Wörgl from the rampaging Waffen-SS. Gangl decided that the best way to accomplish all three objectives was to get the Americans to Wörgl as quickly as possible.

In a bold move, he decided to head for the nearby town of Kufstein to seek the aid of U.S. troops. Riding in a military Kübelwagen driven by a Corporal Keblitsch, Sepp rode through several roadblocks manned by Wehrmacht and Waffen-SS troops. The vehicle had a large white flag of surrender flapping in the breeze. The Kübelwagen is a German light military vehicle designed by Ferdinand Porsche and built by Volkswagen. A forerunner of today's Humvee, it means "bucket car" in English.

The Kübelwagen
Courtesy CC-BY-SA-2.5

The situation was increasingly chaotic and dangerous as they headed closer and closer to the front lines where heavy fighting was still raging. Almost an hour after leaving Wörgl, the Kübelwagen made its way into the center of Kufstein. Flying a white flag was a risky act since it could give a signal to both sides. The Allies would see it as an act of contrition, which was good. The Nazis would see it as an act of betrayal, which was bad. It could cost the major and the corporal their lives.

Driving around a corner they were suddenly face-to-face with a group of four American M4 Sherman tanks that belonged to a reconnaissance unit of the 23rd Tank Battalion of the 12th Armored Division, under the command of Captain John Lee, Jr. In early 1943 the division adopted the nickname "The Hellcats," symbolizing its toughness and readiness for combat. The tanks idled in the town's main plaza while waiting for the 12th to be relieved by the 36th Infantry Division.

The two German soldiers were ordered out of their vehicle by American sentries, put on their knees, and thoroughly searched. In broken English, Major Gangl introduced himself to Captain Lee. The American GI, a football player in high school, was an imposing figure, frequently seen with a cigar in his mouth, and always seen with a forty-five caliber pistol in his holster. This meeting between two former enemies - Major Gangl and Captain Lee - would set the stage for the Battle of Castle Itter.

On the morning of May 4, 1945, just three days after his promotion to captain, Lee had led B Company across the German border into Kufstein. After clearing the town of enemy resistance, U.S. troops were hoping that this would be the last battle they would have to fight. Hitler was dead and Berlin had fallen, so everyone knew that the war could end at any moment. No one wanted to be the last one killed in a war that was already won, and many had their hearts set simply on getting home. The sudden appearance of Major Gangl and his driver from the nearby town of Wörgl changed all that.

Gangl cautiously pulled a letter from his pocket and handed it to Captain Lee. It was the same letter that Andréas Krobot had attempted to deliver to U.S. troops. After quickly skimming it, Lee jumped back in his tank to radio Battalion headquarters. His superior, Lieutenant Colonel Kelso Clow told him, "Use your best judgment and handle the situation however you see fit."

Lee thought for a moment, "Should I trust this Wehrmacht officer?" In the next couple of days, he would replay Clow's words many times in his mind - "Use your best judgment" and "Handle the situation however you see fit."

He looked Gangl in the eyes and then decided he was going to commit all the way with him. He showed his faith in the major by giving him a very unofficial "free pass" in case he was stopped by the Allied authorities. He addressed the following hand-written note to Lieutenant Colonel Clow, figuring that, in the midst of all the chaos, if it was written to and from an American officer, there would be a good chance the major would not be detained. He was now fully committed to Sepp. The message that was torn from a dog-eared pocket-size notebook that Lee carried with him is shown on the following page:

> To: Lt. Col. Clow
> This Major is okay – he is
>   doing a job vital to our
>   cause – let him pass on.
> From: Cpt. John C. Lee

Ch. 7 - The American Captain

Just two weeks earlier, on April 19, Captain Lee had been awarded the Bronze Star at the battle of Strasbourg for "superior leadership ability, cool and aggressive handling of the platoon, and his courage and his ability to meet any situation that confronted him." 27

He was about to be tested by a situation which no American officer had ever had to face.

Captain John C. Lee, Jr.
Courtesy bbc.com/news/world-europe-32622651

"Jack," as he was known to his troops, wasn't quite ready to try to liberate the former Prime Ministers of France and other VIP's. He wanted to complete his assigned task of collecting German prisoners. Having Major Gangl traveling with him proved to be an advantage. Lee's method was simple. With a row of tanks behind him, he drove down the road. When he encountered enemy troops, he just announced that the war was over, which would soon actually be the case for that area. When the troops saw American and German officers in the same jeep, they assumed that what they were being told must be true. There were hundreds who surrendered that day.

The 12th Armored Division official after-action report filed the next morning contained the following account:

> "Lee and the German major stopped at each group of the enemy soldiers, told them that the war was over and that 60 American tanks and a thousand American infantrymen would arrive at Wörgl within the next half-hour. He succeeded in getting the enemy soldiers to lay down their arms and abandon five 88 MM guns as well as having them move the 88 MM ammunition a considerable distance from the guns." 28

Captain Lee was a battle-hardened twenty-seven-year-old from Norwich, New York. He was the commander of a 5-man tank crew that operated an M4A3E8 Sherman nicknamed "Besotten Jenny." The word "Besotten" means "lovesick" or "infatuated."

The "Besotten Jenny"
Courtesy "World of Tanks"

Captain Lee also served as the commanding officer of B Company, 23rd Tank Battalion of the 12th Armored Division. He was a tough, gritty soldier with a penchant for drinking alcohol and smoking cigars.

Born in a small mid-western town in Nebraska, Lee's family moved to rural New York. He was a star football player at Norwich High School. He did well academically but excelled as an athlete and team leader. Lee was accepted into Norwich University in Vermont, one of the largest private military academies in the United States. Once again, he was a standout player with the school football team. He also showed great potential as a cavalry officer in a course that taught cadets how to ride and fight on horseback. Jack developed a passion for tanks after riding in armored vehicles at the parade grounds where the cavalrymen trained. Lee quickly learned to apply the same tactics of the cavalry to armored warfare.

On May 11, 1942, Jack graduated from Norwich and was commissioned a 2nd Lieutenant. He was sent to the armored warfare school in Fort Knox, Kentucky to attend a three-month training course for officers and barely had enough time to marry his wife Virginia back home before he left. After completion of training at Fort Knox, Lieutenant Lee was assigned to the 12th Armored Division based out of Camp Barkeley in Abeline, Texas and given command of a platoon in B Company, 23rd Tank Battalion. After a brief stint in England, the 12th Armored arrived in Le Havre, France on November 11, 1944.

Assigned to the U.S. Seventh Army, the 12th Armored Division would take part in savage fighting in the Alsace-Lorraine region along the French-German Border. Lieutenant Lee was given command of B Company after the previous commander was killed by a land mine on December 9. Lee turned into a hardened combat leader during the bloody campaign in Alsace-Lorraine. He would continue to lead B Company during the Invasion of Germany, earning numerous awards and citations for bravery, including a Bronze Star. Lee consistently impressed his superiors with his natural leadership skills, his tactical expertise, and his ability to seize the initiative. He came to be regarded as one of the best tank commanders in the U.S. Army and paperwork was submitted to promote him to captain.

An incident just after arriving in Kufstein gives insight into Lee's boldness. He was still wearing his First Lieutenant's bar on his collar because his promotion had not yet come through. A German Colonel wanted to surrender his entire battalion but refused to do it to a lowly First Lieutenant. Lee simply glued another bar on his collar so that he would appear to be a captain with two silver bars. The colonel was then willing to surrender his troops. How many other officers would have the audacity to do the simple thing that Lee did?

Jack decided to first recon the area around Itter so he told Major Gangl that he wanted to accompany him in his Kübelwagen to Wörgl and Itter. Lee also brought along his tank gunner, Corporal Edward "Stinky" Szymczyk, and together they headed off with Major Gangl and his driver, Corporal Keblitsch.

Riding in the backseat, the two American GI's had their weapons ready for any ambushes or traps that lay ahead. The "Kübelwagen" passed several groups of Wehrmacht troops along the way, all of whom were known to Major Gangl. They arrived in Wörgl late in the afternoon to find that the Waffen-SS had just recently abandoned the area. Gangl's troops and the Austrian Resistance were now in control of Wörgl.

With Captain Lee's arrival, the Germans formally surrendered authority of the town to the U.S. Army. Realizing the possibility that the SS troops could return, Lee allowed his newfound German allies to keep their weapons. Major Gangl introduced Captain Lee to Rupert Hagleitner, the leader of the local Austrian Resistance in the

Wörgl area, who dressed in civilian clothes and wore a red and white armband. Together they made plans to liberate the prisoners at Castle Itter.

Lee, Szymczyk, Gangl, Hagleitner, and a squad of Wehrmacht troops drove off for Itter. It took them nearly an hour to reach the village as they carefully maneuvered around roadblocks set up by the Waffen-SS. As they entered the center of Itter, they happened to run into Captain Kurt Siegfried Schrader who was heading back to his house after his meeting with the French. Fortunately, Major Gangl knew him from his time in Battle Group Giehl and reassured Captain Lee that the former Waffen-SS officer was on their side.

Lee thought again of the unique situation he was in having to commit himself to not only teaming up with a Wehrmacht major but now also a Waffen-SS captain. Why was the captain to be trusted? Because the major vouched for him? This scenario wasn't covered in officer training school. It wasn't covered in any school. Lee was prepared to "wing it" and hope that his instincts proved right.

According to Schrader:

> "I told Major Gangl, who had joined the resistance movement with some soldiers of his German unit, that I had taken over the security of the French prisoners and asked for military protection. On the spur of the moment Hagleitner had led the two officers to Itter. When I returned with my family shortly afterwards, the French women had made a tri-color and attached it to the castle tower next to a white flag. Both flags

were visible from afar. When I told the French about my meeting with the American officer, everyone hoped, albeit with mixed feelings, for a good ending."
29

At Castle Itter, two French VIP's acting as armed guards witnessed the Kübelwagen coming up the road with a white flag. Word quickly spread. There was sudden excitement running through the castle with news that a U.S. Army officer had been spotted riding up to the castle. Jack met with the honor prisoners and reassured them that he would return shortly and "bring the calvary" to rescue them. Things seemed to be looking up at Castle Itter.

A squad of Major Gangl's troops was left to safeguard the fortress from any attacks by the Waffen-SS. As strange as it sounds, Germans were left to defend the castle in the event of a German attack. Meanwhile Captain Lee and Corporal Szymczyk rushed back to Kufstein. For the time being, the defense of Castle Itter was left under the sole command of former Waffen-SS officer Captain Schrader.

Thanks to Zvonimir Čučković, the relief force from Innsbruck comprising troops from the 103rd Infantry Division led by Major John T. Kramers was already making its way to the castle, but it would still take time for them to arrive. Until then the 23rd Tank Battalion was the closest American unit to assist.

Once back at Battalion HQ in Kufstein, Lee did not hesitate to volunteer to lead the rescue mission, which would be called "Operation Lee." He gathered his men together from Company B and enthusiastically announced, "We're going on a rescue mission!" He then asked, "Who wants to come?"

If it were the beginning of the war, Lee's question would likely have been met with an eager response. Company B, nicknamed the "Hell for Leather" platoon, took on the persona of Lee himself. They were regarded as the most "rough and ready" soldiers in the company.

But this was the war's end. There were assorted groans and moans from the exhausted troops who tried to avoid eye contact with him. That caused him to "volunteer" several people and also seek help from other units willing to spare a few soldiers. Captain Lee continued to scrape together a relief force from whatever resources he could find. Colonel George E. Lynch, commander of the 142nd Infantry Regiment, had assured him that he would shortly be sending out the Regiment's 2nd Battalion to join Lee's small force.

Just after 7 p.m, the rag-tag outfit of American GI's left Kufstein for Itter. Leading the column was Captain Lee, commanding his beloved Sherman tank "Besotten Jenny." Right behind him was his close friend, 33-year-old First Lieutenant Harry J. Basse, who was in charge of a tank named "Boche Buster." "Boche" is a derogatory slang expression which refers to German soldiers. It is believed to be a derivation of the French word, *Caboche*, or "Cabbage."

Taken two months before their deployment to Austria, the photo below shows Company B commander Jack Lee (at left) and motor officer Harry Basse:

Courtesy Blogspot

Lee was also able to acquire the services of three additional M4 Sherman tanks from the 753rd Tank Battalion, along with three squads of infantrymen from the 142nd Infantry Regiment. Not long after leaving Kufstein, the relief force experienced a significant setback.

Jack's column had to cross an old bridge over a tributary of the Inn River. Four of the 66,000-pound tanks made it across the rickety bridge, but as the fifth attempted to cross, the structure quivered and then collapsed. Captain Lee was forced to press on without his infantry support which he chose to leave behind to protect the tank. He was then accompanied by just 14 American soldiers,

Gangl, his driver, and a truck carrying ten former German artillerymen under Gangl's command. As they neared the castle, they engaged, and drove off, a party of SS troops that had been attempting to set up a roadblock. The remnant of Lee's column reached Wörgl at 8pm.

According to Levin,

> "A band of Austrian patriots had liberated Wörgl, and, when they saw the American tanks, their excitement made the whole thing seem more like France than Germany. The Austrians hailed Lee with wine and flowers. The Nazis had fled, they told him. Now all that remained was to liberate the important prisoners in the Castle of Itter, eight kilometers up a side road." 30

To Lee's frustration, though, the Austrian Resistance insisted that he leave behind several more of his tanks to help protect the town from marauding bands of die-hard Waffen-SS troops that were still roving though the countryside. Captain Lee needed as much help as possible to secure the castle but, on the other hand, he knew there wasn't time to waste arguing with the Austrians. Just then Major Gangl stepped in to propose a solution.

Sepp offered to supplement the relief force with some of his loyal Wehrmacht troops if Captain Lee agreed to leave behind several of his tanks. Reluctantly, Lee accepted the offer. American and German soldiers were about to serve together in a World War II joint military operation. Two M4 Sherman tanks were left behind to protect the main road leading into Wörgl. Meanwhile the relief force headed off for Castle Itter now consisted of two Sherman tanks, fourteen U.S. soldiers, and ten German Wehrmacht troops.

Along the way, Captain Lee left the "Boche Buster" to guard a strategic bridge. Lt. Harry Basse, not wanting to miss out on the rescue adventure, volunteered to accompany Lee on the "Besotten Jenny." He gave command of the "Bosche Buster" to Lt. Wallace Holbrook. The latter tank crew remained to protect the bridge and remove some demolition charges that were left behind by the Waffen-SS. The fact that the bridge had been wired to explode was certainly of concern. The Americans knew that likely increased the odds that there was, indeed, going to be an invasion of the castle.

Just outside the village of Itter, the small relief force encountered a roadblock manned by a squad of Waffen-SS troopers. The Allied soldiers opened fire, forcing the small enemy force to scatter into the nearby woods. That night Lee's column drove through Itter and up to the castle.

Captain Lee cautiously turned his tank around and backed it up the narrow 60-foot road leading to the castle so that it would face forward against a potential SS advance. There wasn't room to turn the tank around and he couldn't leave the tank's rear, the most vulnerable part, exposed to the enemy. The tank's rear-view mirror was broken which made the backing-up procedure that much more difficult. A mistake would have been catastrophic. The tank could have easily plunged into the deep ravine on either side.

The Road Leading to Castle Itter
Courtesy Atlas Obscura

He left the "Besotten Jenny" parked on the small bridge, where it commanded the entrance to the castle. The heavy doors suddenly swung open and an excited and delighted company of distinguished-looking gentlemen began pouring out of the castle.

Seeing the American rescuers, the French cheered wildly and held up bottles of wine in eager anticipation of their formal liberation. But the jubilation soon turned to disappointment as the French looked upon the meager size of the force sent to rescue them.

Earlier that day, Captain Lee had promised them that he would bring "the cavalry" to their aid. The French whispered to each other, "This is what the captain brought us? More Germans?" They had expected an American column of armor supported by a mass of infantry troops. What they got was a lone tank, seven Americans from random units, and a truckload of a dozen disaffected German troops.

Unimpressed by the small task force, they kept asking, "Where are the rest of the soldiers?" and "One tank? That's all you have?" In particular, some expressed disdain for Captain Lee. Former Prime Minister Daladier, in fact, called him "crude in both looks and manners." "If Lee is a reflection of America's policies," he added, "Europe is in for a hard time." On the other hand, he admired Gangl, describing him as "polite" and "dignified." 31

Imagine two former Prime Ministers and two retired Generals of the Army of France being asked to take orders from a brash 27-year-old American who had just been promoted from First Lieutenant to Captain days earlier. They all would have expected Lee to defer to them and follow their orders. That, however, was not Lee's mindset. To him, this was, and would remain, "Operation Lee" with all that implied.

The French imprisoned in the castle knew they were in grave danger. They told each other that this handful of American and German soldiers along with a lone tank defending the castle was not likely to make much of a difference at all.

The 12th Infantry Division after-action report filed that day had this grim entry - "The group was in great fear because they anticipated being murdered by SS troops before the American troops arrived." 32

Ch. 8 - Preparing for Battle

Jack Lee had never heard of the Castle Itter but was eager to liberate prisoners of the Germans. The "Besotten Jenny" and its small relief force finally arrived safely at the Alpine fortress.

According to Schrader:

> "I gathered the French now and officially handed them over to the American officer. My mission was fulfilled, but Captain Lee asked me to stay at the castle until further reinforcements would come, as he still feared German attacks. So, I spent the night with my family in the castle." 33

Later that evening, Schrader reported to Lee that some of Gangl's men had sighted enemy forces moving within the vicinity. Realizing that an attack could come at any moment, Lee asked the former prisoners to seek shelter in the castle cellars. That drew outrage from several of the French who pledged to die fighting rather than cower in a basement.

Not intimidated by the honor prisoners, Lee lectured them saying, "You have a duty to help rebuild France after the war and your deaths would not do their nation any good." As most, but not all, of the French dignitaries, reluctantly agreed to stay in the cellars, American and German officers held a meeting to organize defenses for the castle.

Captain Lee realized that they held fortified positions on the high ground, and the thick walls of the castle would provide significant protection from small arms fire. If enemy troops attacked from the north, south, or west, they would have to exhaust themselves scaling the sides of the hill under heavy fire. If they attacked from the east, they would be exposed traveling up the main road. They felt it was only a matter of time before additional U.S. troops arrived, so they intended to try to hold out until relief came.

The German soldiers tied a dark piece of cloth around their left arms to distinguish themselves as friendlies for the coming battle. The American soldiers disparagingly referred to their German Allies as "Tame Krauts." "Kraut" is a derogatory term for Germans referring to sauerkraut. Lee, Basse, Gangl, and Schrader each commanded a section of the castle's perimeter. "Besotten Jenny" was parked in front of the gatehouse overlooking the main road as the first line of defense. Armed with a 76mm cannon capable of firing 20 rounds/minute, a .50-caliber machine gun, and two .30-caliber machine guns, the tank covered the approach to the castle.

That night, Captain Lee, Major Gangl, and Captain Schrader walked around making a thorough inspection of the castle defenses and agreed on tactics. Positioning the "Besotten Jenny" at the castle entrance made it clearly visible from the valley side. It was hoped that the presence of the tank would help discourage attackers. Then they headed down into the cellars to inform those huddled there of their plans.

Afterwards, the three officers sat together at dinner in the castle's great hall and shared talk of their war experiences. Despite the fact that they had fought on opposing sides, the German officers found they had a lot in common with the American captain. In turn, the Wehrmacht and SS officer quickly developed a friendship. They were just three soldiers laughing and joking as they dined and drank together. For a few hours, they were able to put aside the sense of dread they were all feeling. Little did they know the fate that would befall one of the trio within the next several hours.

After dinner, the Americans, Germans, and French then invaded the wine cellar and did something hard to imagine. They had a party in a medieval castle that was about to be invaded by Nazi soldiers with the intent of assassinating them.

According to Levin:

> "Captain Lee and his soldiers relaxed and celebrated with the generals and politicians who staged a farewell dinner with wine and many toasts in the gloomy, narrow-windowed dining room where they had passed so many hours of the last years together, politely avoiding the dangerous subject of France's defeat, for that would have led only to recriminations between them. Yes, it was quite an exciting evening. Beds were found for the boys but in the morning, they were awakened by a familiar sound. They were being shot at." 34

Ch. 9 - The Battle

It would turn out to be a very short night for the castle defenders. At 4 a.m., Captain Lee was awakened by loud, strange cracking sounds. He lifted his head up and saw chips of stone splintering off the wall. Jack quickly realized that the grand celebration the night before had been a bit premature. His troops were running around cursing as gunfire broke out around the castle.

The attackers were the 17th Waffen-SS Panzer Grenadier Division led by Obenführer George Bochmann. They had been retreating from Wörgl in the direction of Kitzbühel. Although depleted, the force still consisted of more than enough troops to overwhelm the castle defenders. Estimates on their numbers range from 150 to 200 soldiers, about the size of a typical company. Schrader had thought he had taken off his Waffen-SS uniform for good. Instead, he quickly donned it again in case he was asked to approach the enemy to negotiate with them.

The focus of the initial attack was to assess the strength of the defending troops and probe the fortress for weaknesses. The enemy was testing the defenses, seeking a way to penetrate the castle without launching what they felt could result in a costly all-out assault.

Moonlight provided enough illumination to discern outlines but little else. With nervous eyes, the Allies were looking out the castle windows, searching for movement in the blackened landscape. It was made all the more frightening by the fact that heightened senses tend to play tricks on the mind. Anyone who has been in a night-time battle knows the feeling.

"Save your ammo, wait until you see something definite," Lee cautioned. A veteran of many skirmishes, the American captain tried his best to calm the castle defenders.

A German MG-42 machine gun started pelting the fortress from a parallel ridge line to the east. The first American shots were fired by Sergeant William Rushford using the tank's .50 caliber Browning. PFC's Herbert McHaley and Alfred Worsham used "Besotten Jenny's" .30 caliber Browning to suppress enemy fire coming from the top floor of a nearby Inn in Itter.

Manning one of the towers, Corporal William Sutton spotted several Waffen-SS cutting through the barbed wire which surrounded the castle. They then attempted to scale the castle wall with grappling hooks and ropes. Firing his M-1 Garand rifle into their midst, Sutton caused the infiltrators to climb back down the wall and flee down the slope.

Captain Lee moved through the castle checking the defenses, as American and German troops began opening fire upon the shadowy figures and muzzle flashes around the vicinity.

A major issue arose as gunfire erupted near the gatehouse around 8 a.m. One of the Allied German soldiers had taken off down the ravine and into the forest, apparently defecting to the enemy. An American, PFC Arthur Pollack, fired his BAR machine gun (M1918 Browning Automatic Rifle) at him but missed.

The friendly German had evidently changed his mind about surrendering and feared being captured and killed for treason. He then may simply have run away or, worse yet, may have joined the SS and, to try to win their favor, given them information about the force, or lack of force, in the castle. This, naturally, caused Lee to worry about the loyalty of the remaining German soldiers.

Through Major Gangl, Jack demanded to know how the defector was allowed to escape and questioned why none of the German Allies opened fire on him. Lee wondered if they were afraid to shoot at another German. If that were true, would they really fight against their fellow countrymen in the Waffen-SS? Was the escapee an outlier or representative of the other friendly Germans?
Just how "friendly" were they, really? Where did their loyalty lie? Would they really be willing to give their lives to save a bunch of elite French prisoners? All these thoughts were racing through Lee's mind.

Gangl speculated that the soldier panicked and wanted to avoid execution in the event that they were overrun. Afterwards, the major went around the castle ensuring his men that their only hope was to stick with their American allies. He assured them that if they did, they would survive the war. Sepp reported back to Captain Lee, promising that he and his men would carry on the fight to its conclusion. Jack hesitated for a moment but then realized he had to trust that Gangl could keep his troops in line. He needed them. He simply had no other option.

The initial exchange of gunfire lasted for only ten minutes and then it stopped. Lee wondered whether the enemy really wanted the castle or whether they simply saw the tank out front and were seeking some sort of token revenge or just letting off pent-up anger before moving on. He, of course, was hoping for the latter because he knew they didn't have enough ammunition to hold off a sustained attack. He didn't have to wait long to find the answer.

A second attack, much more potent than the first, began around 8:30 a.m. Schrader reported matter-of-factly, "Flak rounds struck the castle turret, and my wife, who threw herself over our children in a protective manner, was slightly injured by falling stones." Bleeding from several cuts on her forehead and neck, she wasn't the only one wondering how much more blood would be shed that day. The captain then added, "All feared the worst." 35

The battle was raging. The glass windows of the castle were shot out. Chunks of masonry fell all around as the assault continued. Sepp Gangl reported seeing approximately 150 SS-Waffen troops dismounting from a column of trucks on the Ittererstasse, Itter's main street.

Hearing sounds of a German MP-40 sub-machine gun downstairs, Captain Lee and Major Gangl went into a room to find a friendly

German soldier lying on the floor wounded. The two officers pulled the man to safety while under heavy fire. The young soldier explained that he saw a group of Waffen-SS penetrating the barbed wire defenses, and emptied an entire clip from his MP-40, forcing the enemy to fall back. No enemy troops had yet reached the walls of the castle. According to Levin:

> "It was a bright, warm morning. There was peppery intermittent fire. General Gamelin, looking dandy and neat, with brightly polished leather leggings, decided to take his morning constitutional in the courtyard, regardless. As he paced briskly behind the battlements, an 88 plowed into the roof of the castle, exploding squarely in the general's room. He trotted up the stairs and gazed upon the wreckage, which was complete. He had been lucky. Yes, a narrow escape. Oddly, it cheered him up - something like old times." 36

Captain Lee climbed to the top of the keep observing the area through his binoculars and was troubled by what he saw. Waffen-SS troops were swarming through the area. He also spotted two 20mm anti-aircraft guns along with an 88mm artillery gun being set up nearby. The intention of the enemy troops converging on the medieval fortress was brutally clear - eliminate all of the occupants. No one knew whether those orders came directly from Himmler or were initiated by Waffen-SS Division Commander Bochmann. No one knew, either, whether it was a carefully planned or simply an ad-hoc operation. None of this really mattered to the castle defenders who, along with the VIP's, were in mortal danger.

Battle Damage to Castle Itter
Courtesy British Broadcasting Company

If the Waffen-SS troops were to breach the outer ramparts after the defenders used all of their ammunition, the plan was to fight to the death in medieval-style combat. It wouldn't be much of a match, of course, with the small Allied contingent against an overwhelming SS force. Lee gathered the castle defenders together and announced, "If the battle goes the wrong way, everyone abandon their positions and, if necessary, muster in the central keep to fight hand-to-hand."

Major Gangl called Alois Mayr, an Austrian Resistance leader in Wörgl via the castle's telephone and pleaded with him to get word out to any U.S. Army units nearby that those within the fortress were in dire need of assistance. An hour later, the American-German garrison received several reinforcements. Two more Wehrmacht soldiers loyal to Major Gangl along with a 17-year-old Austrian

Resistance fighter named Hans Woltl rode from Wörgl sneaking past Waffen-SS troopers to get to their besieged comrades. Needless to say, the addition of three men wasn't going to tilt the scales in favor of the Allies.

Soon the castle was being struck as an 88mm Flak 37 and a 20 mm Flak 30, situated approximately 700 meters northwest of the castle opened fire on the defenders. The woods surrounding the castle erupted with automatic weapons fire, marking the beginning of the main assault on the castle.

Daladier hid out in one of the second-floor bedrooms, where two of the German Wehrmacht soldiers took up positions with their rifles resting on the window sills. The former Prime Minister recalled:

> "They pointed out SS troops firing at the castle from a few hundred yards away, near the little electric plant, on the edge of the forest. The two soldiers returned the fire. I took advantage of a moment of calm to exchange a few words with our defenders. They told me in German that they were Polish. When I told them I was French, one of them started shaking my hand while the other pulled a bottle out of his coat and offered it to me. It was a bottle of Fernet Branca; where the devil did he get that? I drank a bit; it was really bad. Then he laughed and told me Hitler was kaput. 37

The first Allied casualty of the attack was the "Besotten Jenny." Around 10:30 a.m. during the lull in the fighting, Private First Class Art Pollock and Al Worsham were sitting behind "Besotten Jenny," smoking cigarettes and nervously watching for enemy troop movement.

The two soldiers were protecting Technician Fourth Grade Bill Rushford, who was inside the tank working to repair the radio that had gone out of commission somewhere on the road between Wörgl and Itter. They were suddenly shocked by the blast of anti-tank rounds hitting the M4 Sherman followed by a loud metallic clang.

PFC's Providing Security
Courtesy wallpapertag.com

The tank lurched backward and then forward on its suspension. Knowing that at any moment enemy troops could emerge from the nearby trees, Pollock was frantically looking for his partner when he heard Worsham yelling, 'Pollock, Pollock, are you dead?'

"How the hell am I gonna answer you if I'm dead?" he responded. "Hell no, I'm not dead!"

"Come underneath the bridge and up the other side. I'm over there," Worsham shouted. 38

Pollock hurried through the opening and found the rifleman waiting on the other side. Together the two GIs scrambled awkwardly uphill to the castle entryway, pounding on it and yelling until it was opened enough for them to squeeze through. To their amazement, the man opening the door was Rushford. They had assumed he was dead.

The enemy round had penetrated the tank's armor and gone through the crew compartment, just missing Rushford's right leg, but destroying the engine. Rushford was standing inside the vehicle, facing the radio set rack at the rear of the turret when the round hit. Although dazed, he had the presence of mind to swing open the hatch and climb up through the turret, then run as fast as he could to the castle's front gate.

Itter Castle Door
Courtesy Steve Morgan/CC BY-SA-3.0

Harry Basse was manning the gate, opening it for him just as the "Besotten Jenny's" fuel tanks caught fire and exploded. Miraculously, Rushford survived the incident and was unhurt. But, Captain Lee's "Besotten Jenny," and the castle's top weapon, was turned into a fiery inferno.

The Germans, unfortunately, had discovered early in the war that Shermans were prone to catching on fire when hit in the fuel tanks. When the Shermans appeared in battle, the Germans would sometimes call out, "Here come the Ronsons!" That, of course, refers to the famous American cigarette lighter.

While all this was occurring, French VIP's Paul Reynaud, Francois de la Rocque, Michael Clemenceau, Maurice Gamelin, and Jean Borotra had disregarded Lee's orders and were out and about roaming the castle, despite the battle taking place around them. They felt they could not stand idly by while Allied troops were fighting desperately to hold off the enemy.

According to Reynaud:

> "I soon saw that, as the tank was burning, the attackers could penetrate from the other side into the courtyard by the bridge which linked up with the flank of the mountain. I dodged into the castle. I got my tommy-gun out of my trunk and went down to the courtyard, where I found some soldiers. Clemenceau had already calmly posted himself at a loophole in case the attackers wished to take possession of the tank. I took up a position near to him." 39

The Allied troops shot from behind the protection of the parapets. Some of the prisoners, though, were ignoring Lee's orders to keep their heads down. Ex-Prime Minister Paul Reynaud was in the thick of the fight. Around noon, he began moving into the open eager to fight the enemy. Perhaps getting carried away trying to play soldier, he abandoned cover and exposed himself to enemy fire.

Major Gangl saw that Reynaud was in danger and rushed to grab him and try to move him to safer position. As he ran across the courtyard, Gangl suddenly fell to the ground. He had been struck in the head by a sniper's bullet. His body immediately went limp, blood poured from his head, and he was killed instantly.

Captains Lee and Schrader were stunned by Gangl's death. There was no time, though, for them or any of the others to mourn the loss of their friend as enemy fire was intensifying. Gaping holes suddenly appeared on the castle exterior. The inhabitants began to wonder if the castle walls could withstand the constant pounding of artillery shells.

Renaud felt terribly he was not able to avenge Gangl's death:

> "We ran to the other side of the castle in order to defend the surrounding wall, although the ground fell away in a steep slope. The young Austrian patriot with a white and red brassard (armband) showed himself very active. A Wehrmacht lieutenant, using his binoculars, pointed out targets against which to direct our fire. I regret that I cannot confirm that I killed one enemy." 40

Meanwhile, Major Kramers was still fuming about learning that Itter was outside the boundary of operations for the 103rd Division. He felt he didn't go to all this trouble to turn around now. He reasoned that they had told him to abort the rescue operation but they didn't specifically say that he couldn't take a couple of jeeps to the castle to check things out. Disobeying orders because of a technicality is the kind of action that might make someone a hero if it succeeds. If not, it can get someone a court martial.

The team set out early in the morning, with Major Kramers, Lieutenant Lutten, Čučković, and a Sergeant Gris leading in a jeep. Two civilians - U.S. war correspondent Meyer Levin and French photographer Eric Schwab – asked for and were granted permission to accompany the rescue force to Schloss Itter.

They completed the ride to Wörgl without incident. When they saw the "Bosche Buster," sitting on the road, they let out a sigh of relief. They were briefed by the soldiers and a group of Austrian partisans about Lee's rescue effort and the fact that he left the tank as rear guard.

Kramers' party continued on to Itter Castle and from a safe distance, could see the battle clearly through field glasses. There was a dense pillar of black smoke from the ""Besotten Jenny" as it continued burning. As they watched, the beleaguered castle, surrounded by a division of Waffen-SS soldiers, continued to be pounded by artillery. In the words of Levin, the enemy was "determined to finish them off in one last murder orgy."

It looked like reinforcements had suddenly appeared in true thriller style. Eric Schwab, the photographer, burst into the town hall to inform Kramer and his party that he'd seen an American column approaching from the north. They all leaped into their jeeps and sped out to meet the column and guide them to the castle. When they met the tanks, half-tracks, and infantry, they were dismayed to learn that they knew nothing about defending a beleaguered castle.

According to Levin, one of the officers said, "We're just supposed to travel down this road and link up with the 103$^{rd.}$ That's our mission. We haven't got any order to move out and attack a castle."

"Who's got to give you the order?" Kramers asked.

"Colonel Lynch" was the reply.

"Where's he?"

"He just left us. He's gone back up the road someplace."

They took one of the officers, Lt. Cliff Reinhardt, out of the column to accompany them in the search for Colonel Lynch. About 10 kilometers up the road, Reinhardt yelled, "That's his jeep!" Kramers briefed the colonel about the situation at the castle and he gave Lieutenant Reinhardt immediate authorization for the rescue operation.

After arriving at Wörgl with Reinhardt, Kramers asked the partisans if there was any way to contact Captain Lee.

One of them responded, "Have you tried calling him on the phone?"

Kramers said, "Are you kidding me? I can call him on a regular telephone?"

The resistance fighters indicated there was, indeed, a phone in the town hall and it was feasible that someone would answer in the castle. Kramers tried the line and, to his surprise, was able to get through. In the middle of the fighting, Captain Lee was called to the phone. He reported, "They're shelling the bajabers out of us. Listen, better get some help up here right away." 42

Suddenly the line went dead. There would be no further communication with those trapped in the castle. The phone line had evidently been cut.

American and German soldiers, with the aid of the French VIP's, were holding their own at Castle Itter but were running dangerously low both on ammunition and hope for survival. The Waffen-SS was still unable to breach the castle walls but were attacking with increasing ferocity. While the call from Major Kramers had given some hope to the defenders, the situation was still dire. Captain Lee, unfortunately, hadn't been able to give him any intel on the disposition of enemy forces.

Machine-gun and artillery fire from artillery pieces was coming from all sides. Snipers were closing in. They were shooting from trees only a stone's throw away from the walls. The Allies were expecting the Waffen-SS to storm the castle at any moment and that they would all be slaughtered.

Lee was in just about the most difficult spot he had ever been in. He took stock. Under his command, he had a handful of American soldiers, close to twenty assorted Germans of varying degrees of loyalty, and a few civilians. Meanwhile, he had to hold the line. Surely, help could not be far away.

Around 2 p.m., Jean Borotra stepped forward volunteering to vault over the 15-foot castle walls and run the gauntlet of SS troops. He claimed, "There is no more I can do here now. But I can try to go through their lines and bring help. I want to go and get some reinforcements."

Captain Lee was reluctant to let the tennis player run off telling him, "The odds of your making it out alive are slim to none."

Nevertheless, Borotra was confident. He was always confident, no matter the situation. Even at 47 years old, the audacious tennis star was probably the best qualified for the task. He had made it a daily habit to run around the castle's interior courtyard to maintain his physical conditioning. Thirty minutes later, things were looking more desperate and an impromptu war council was held. Gamelin, Weygand, and Lee all agreed. They accepted Borotra's offer.

Borotra had actually escaped from the castle by vaulting over the wall on three prior occasions. The first was in the fall of 1943 and the second in late March, 1945. Both times he got several miles before being recaptured. He was not executed. In fact, he was simply confined to his room for a few days.

The third attempt, on April 29, 1945, came just a week before the Battle of Castle Itter. At about 6:30 p.m. that night, Daladier was strolling in the castle's rear courtyard when he saw the tennis player, who greeted him with "Have a nice walk, Prime Minister."

According to Daladier:

"Borotra ran to south wall, scaled it, and started running madly down the hill. The SS guards began firing at him from a few yards away. He took the barbed wire in stride as more and more shots rang out and the SS began their pursuit. At 7:20 P.M. Borotra was brought back. He had probably twisted an ankle, given the way he was limping." 43

Borotra's only punishment again was just a few days of house arrest. It evidently helped to be a world-famous athlete.

Jean had some wild experiences in his career on the tennis court. This day, May 5, he would have what would undoubtedly be his wildest off-court experience. Jean's performance would include multiple costume changes. As in so many of his matches, when all seemed lost, he would be triumphant in the end.

Ch. 10 - The Tennis Player

Born in Biarritz, Aquitaine, Jean Borotra developed hand-eye coordination as a boy by playing a game called Basque Pelota, made popular in the Basque area of France. Reminiscent of racquetball, it's a court sport played with a ball using your hand, racket, or wooden bat against a wall. Jean didn't actually begin to play tennis until he was 14 years old. He developed his signature style of playing forehands from both sides and charging the net as often as he could. His fierce sense of competition soon made him a tough opponent, although, according to his own words, even at his best, he "only knew how to smash, volley and maybe hit a backhand." 44

Jean Borotra
Courtesy of the Bibliothèque Nationale, Paris

Jean's difficulty with his backhand didn't prevent him from rising to the top of the tennis world. His strength was his aggressive style.

He would serve the ball and rush the net so fast that the ball would often come very close to hitting him on the back of the head.

His tennis career was interrupted at 18 years of age when he joined the French Army to fight in World War I. He was awarded the Croix de Guerre for bravery. After returning home, he graduated from the Polytechnique school in Paris, while continuing to work on his tennis skills. As early as 1921, he showed his potential by winning a match against one of the top French players, André Gobert.

The "Bounding Basque"
Courtesy Bundesarchiv, Bild 102-10990 / CC BY-SA 3.0 de

In an illustrious career, Jean went on to win 18 major championships including four Grand Slam men's singles titles (Wimbledon twice, the Australian Open, and French Open.) Showing remarkable versatility, he also won nine men's doubles and five mixed doubles tournaments. By 1930, he was ranked as the best player in the world. Along with René Lacoste, Henri Cochet, and Toto Brugnon, he was one of the "Four Musketeers" from France who dominated tennis in the late 1920's and early 1930's. They helped their country win six straight Davis Cups from 1927 to 1932, defeating the United States five times. In 1933, Borotra said that "Being part of the Musketeers was one of my greatest joys. We had a marvelous camaraderie." 45

Jean might have enjoyed the game but, above all, he loved the showmanship. Tournament referee Frank Burrows recalls that "He laughed so much in the middle of his own jokes that you couldn't hear the end of them." 46

An inordinate number of his matches would follow the same script. He'd take an early lead, let the opponent back in the match, and then close out, much to the delight of the crowd, with a breathtaking rally at the end. He'd take a bow and celebrate a narrow victory. Whether he did this on purpose or not was a subject of debate among tennis experts. One thing for sure. He knew how to entertain a crowd.

Borotra may have been the greatest matinee idol that tennis has ever produced. Spectators would flock to see him in action. In his long white flannel pants and his signature beret, he'd rush into the net and produce acrobatic volleys which had his admirers "Ooh!" and "Ah!" with delight. Even in his toughest matches he would catch the eye of pretty girls on the sidelines and smile at them. Much to the annoyance of his opponents, he'd even kiss a few of their hands between points.

The British newspaper, *The Independent,* compared his matches to "theatrical productions." Borotra had a flair for the dramatic — on wide shots he'd tumble into the stands. In best 3-of-5 sets, he'd bring five blue or black berets and rotate the hats at critical moments in the match. He would chat with fans and then get serious and flick a switch at will and become dominant. Jean's showmanship on the court added to his celebrity status. Long and lean at 6-foot-1 and 160 pounds, his legs were like springs. A whirlwind on the court, Jean played the game at a frenetic pace — diving, tumbling, jumping. His hard-charging approach to tennis earned him the nickname, "The Bounding Basque."

Jean would dance back and forth across between entertainment and gamesmanship, breaking opponents' concentration and then unleashing his trademark overhead smashes. American Bill Tilden, a fierce competitor who won 14 major singles titles himself, paid him begrudging compliments by saying, "Borotra was unquestionably the most difficult man to play against" 47 and "He was the god of galleries and devil of the players." 48

You can imagine a scene with him as a child looking up at his mother and saying, "When I grow up, I want to be a tennis player" and she'd respond, "Sorry, Jean, you can't do both." It turned out he stayed a playful child while also becoming the top-ranked tennis player in the world.

A member of François de la Rocque's *Parti Social Francais* ("French Social Party"), Berotra was named 1st General Commissioner for Education and Sports, serving from August 1940 to April 1942.

When World War II broke out, Jean made a choice that would prove to haunt him. He threw his support behind Phillippe Pétain and what would become the Vichy government. He expressed anger when instructed that he could not put French Jews on the teams he organized. He was summoned to the German embassy in Paris where he refused to exclude "undesirables" from French sports programs. The Nazis ordered him fired from his position.

In 1942, he decided to attempt to try to escape to North Africa and join the Allied cause. He was picked up by the Gestapo, though, within minutes of his arrival at a Paris train station. He was taken into custody and, over the next seven days, pumped full of sodium pentathol, a truth serum, while being interrogated.

He spent six months in a solitary cell at the Nazi prison camp in Sachsenhausen, outside of Berlin. He had no running water or toilet available. Learning of his dire situation, one of the four Musketeers, René Lacoste, petitioned the King of Sweden, an acquaintance and avid tennis fan, to intervene on Borotra's behalf. King Gustav had enough pull with Adolph Hitler to get Jean transferred to the comfortable confines of Itter Castle. He termed the two years he spent at Itter as "paradise" compared to life in a concentration camp.

According to the French newspaper, *Le Monde*, the Bounding Basque imagined himself dying on the tennis court and not in a concentration camp or on the battlefield. Jean pictured his end coming this way: "I come to the net. My opponent hits a huge lob.

On that lob, I hit an unstoppable shot into the opposite corner and collapse on the court with my arms crossed. And forever."

British tennis great Fred Perry admired Borotra's tenacity. He once said, "Jean Borotra was always prepared to kill himself for France." 45 That may have been an exaggeration when it came to describing him on the tennis court but proved to be literally true when it came to the Battle of Castle Itter.

Would Jean have had regrets if he had died trying to save his fellow Frenchmen at the castle? He once said, "The only possible regret I have is the feeling that I will die without having played enough tennis. 49

So, it had to be Jean. Someone had to step into the limelight. Someone had to save the day. The stage was set. Who else but the ultimate showman would take on the task of completing a seemingly impossible mission?

Boratra's plan was to dress up in the guise of a local peasant. To look the part, he decided to change into traditional knee-length breeches known as "lederhosen.' Because of their durability, these leather garments were worn as work or leisure wear for gardening, hiking, working outdoors, or attending folk festivals. Looking like someone in an Octoberfest costume, Jean combined his lederhosen with high white stockings and a checked shirt. He also carried a bindle, a slang term for a bundle of bedding on a stick, typically carried by a homeless person.

The Frenchman easily scaled the fifteen-foot wall and, after dropping to the ground below, started running toward the nearby woods.

"Jean Borotra was the spark of the defense," Lee recalled. "He volunteered to jump over the castle wall and make his way to Wörgl to summon help. It meant a run over forty yards of open field before he could reach cover." 50

Lee had asked Jean what kind of weapon he wanted to carry. An M-1 would provide him firepower but, on the other hand, a pistol carried in a holster would not impede his movement and would still allow him to defend himself.

"I don't need a weapon. I'm just going to blend in with the scenery." responded Borotra.

"Okay," Lee said, "Have it your way." He didn't want to argue with Jean. He was more focused on keeping the other honor prisoners alive as long as possible.

Borotra made it to the bottom of the hill where he encountered two Waffen-SS troopers manning a MG-42 machine gun. They were caught off guard by his sudden appearance and just stared at him. He waved to them. Walking slowly and casually, he stopped to fill his pipe with tobacco and light up. Jean bent over to examine some mushrooms. Then, to the surprise of the SS soldiers, he stopped to calmly urinate onto a tree. They couldn't help but laugh.

The Frenchman acted in such a casual manner that it confused the storm troopers who, noting he was unarmed, dismissed him as any sort of a threat. One of the enemy soldiers poked the other in the ribs and pointed at Jean saying, "Look at that fool. He doesn't even know he's in the middle of a battle!" The dumbfounded SS troops then simply allowed him to go on his way.

Borotra continued to smile broadly and wave to the other Waffen-SS he encountered. They seemed too amused by his antics to be suspicious. They, too, assumed, that he must be a local innocent, oblivious to what was taking place around him. Maintaining coolness in a pressure-packed situation was something Borotra was used to. It likely saved his life that day.

To reach Wörgl, Jean had to cross a stream. He strolled to the bank and, holding his bindle over his head, carefully walked into the water, struggling to maintain his balance on the rocks. Wet to the waist but still grinning happily, he approached the American lines.

Embedded with the unit was Rene Levesque, a French-Canadian war correspondent who would later become the Premier of Quebec. Levesque noticed one of the American GI's shouting and pointing to a man in drenched civilian clothing running towards them while waving his arms. Gunfire from the castle battle could still be heard in the distance. The GI's, like the Waffen-SS soldiers, thought he was some local peasant but Levesque was shocked when Borotra got closer and he realized who the man was:

> "Being a tennis buff, I recognized him almost immediately. It was Borotra, an all-time champion. He was hardly winded and told us that he'd just walked out of the chateau-prison of Itter a few kilometers up the road." 51

Jean was then directed to a farmhouse where Colonel Marvin Coyle had set up a command post for the 142nd Regiment. Though not currently in the military, Jean knew how to play his role. He marched straight up to Coyle, saluted smartly, and identified himself. Then he told him in a speech he had rehearsed in his mind many times over:

> "My name is Jean Borotra. I was being held captive at Castle Itter. We're under attack by the SS. I've been sent out by Captain John Lee of the 23rd Tank Battalion, 12th Armored Division on an urgent mission to find you and ask for your help. I can give you the German gun positions, which I have seen. I can lead a detail around the back way."

The Colonel knew Jean as the famous tennis player but, more importantly, was eager to have someone who was familiar with the terrain and the positions of the enemy soldiers and artillery. The intelligence he provided was critical. Much to his delight, Jean was allowed to ride in the lead tank of the column that was sent to rescue the castle defenders. The rest of the soldiers moved cautiously behind the other tanks, taking cover while firing their weapons.

Asking to change from his Austrian peasant garb into a regulation U.S. Army uniform, Borotra led elements of E and G Company towards the castle, breaking through enemy defensive positions along a nearby stream. He wasn't sporting his famous tennis beret but instead had on the signature M1 "steel pot" helmet used by U.S. troops during World War II and up until 1985. It was not bullet-proof as many believed but did offer some protection against flying pieces of shrapnel. Along the way, they knocked out several machine-gun nests and narrowly dodged an ambush by a squad with a seventy-five-millimeter gun on a halftrack.

Borotra managed to shoot several Waffen-SS attacking the rescue force. His group also took twelve enemy troops prisoner without suffering any casualties.

So Borotra didn't die on the court as he imagined or on the battlefield, either. He lived to play his last competitive tennis match at the veteran doubles event at Wimbleton at age 87. He passed away quietly in his bed in 1994, just weeks before his 96th birthday.

The final line of his obituary reads, "Jean Borotra was a man with style." That was, indeed, a fitting summation.

Meanwhile, Major Kramers knew that Captain Lee needed help immediately but he didn't have a big enough force to protect the castle prisoners. Suddenly a miraculous sight rolled into Wörgl. Six M4 Sherman tanks from the 753rd Tank Battalion along with troops from the 142nd Infantry Regiment. These were advance units heading to link up with the 103rd Infantry Division and were not aware of the dire situation at Castle Itter. Major Kramers quickly conferred with the company and regimental commanders. They agreed to leave behind three tanks and a platoon to help safeguard the town, while the rest headed off for the nearby castle.

Led by Captain John W. Gill, the relief force had rolled out of Wörgl to the cheers of dozens of now-liberated Austrian citizens. On their way to the castle, the column encountered many beleaguered German soldiers seeking to surrender. Most of these troops had been conscripted into the Wehrmacht. The American GI's disarmed the German soldiers but ordered them to head west while they continued to push forward. As the column moved close to Castle Itter, they encountered increasingly stubborn resistance from the Waffen-SS but they were able to fight their way through.

Lee feared the tankers coming up the road might not realize who was in the castle. They could assume it was still a German stronghold and simply blast away. As the American relief column approached the fortress, Lee conferred with General Weygand, saying, "I have an idea. We've got to let the American troops know who we are." He and Weygard quickly came up with a plan that was the football equivalent of the "Hail Mary" play. They teamed up on a 30-calibre machine gun and opened fire sending long bursts crackling into the woods ahead of the approaching American tanks.

Fortunately, this message was understood. Sergeant William E. Elliot in the lead tank had his ninety-millimeter gun trained on the castle when he recognized the sound of a friendly American machine gun. The relief column, assisted by soldiers from the 36th Infantry Division, broke through enemy lines at 3 p.m. on May 5.

"It worked," sighed Lee. "Later I found out that the tankers had their heavy guns trained on the castle ready to fire when they recognized the sound of an American '30' and decided it was a signal rather than a threat." 52 The possibility of being killed by the would-be American rescuers was averted for Lee and others in the castle.

Lee and Schrader had ordered their troops to pull back to the castle keep in preparation for their last stand. They had finally run out of ammunition. A squad of heavily-armed Waffen-SS began advancing towards the front entrance. One of them pointed his *panzerfaust*, a disposable anti-tank rocket, directly at the gatehouse. The weapon was a precursor of the rocket propelled grenade launcher and would have put a large hole in the solid wooden door. The SS troops were prepared to pour into the castle. The SS assault force decided this was the moment to push forward with an all-out assault.

Waffen-SS Soldier wielding a Panzerfaust
Courtesy WW2-Weapons.com

Then, it happened. Like a miracle. Like it was from an old Western movie. As Lee had promised, the cavalry really did arrive. The timing could not have been better. One of the friendly Germans stationed high in one of the castle towers shouted out, "*Amerikanische Panzer!*" which means "American Tank." It would have been hard to picture a World War II German soldier screaming that out and meaning it in a positive sense. That, however, is the way it happened.

Cannon fire rang out from the German attackers. "Jenny's" sister tank, the "*Boche Buster,*" accompanied by a company of American infantry, was riding to the rescue. They were soon joined by the troops led by Borotra, sporting his crisp, clean, borrowed U.S. Army uniform. He definitely looked the part of a U.S. soldier. Borotra wore the uniform proudly.

Reynaud reported happily, "At length we heard sounds of a skirmish between American tanks coming to our help and the SS. From that moment on, the game was won. That afternoon, we were liberated," 53

The Waffen-SS troopers quickly melted away into the countryside as the U.S. soldiers approached the front gatehouse. Those in the battered fortress cheered. The American, German, French, and Austrian defenders of the castle rushed outside to the front entrance in celebration as a column of M4 Sherman tanks along with truckloads of infantrymen arrived.

The first soldiers to reach the castle defenders were two sergeants, William E. Elliot and Glenn E. Sherman. Captain Lee walked out to greet them. He didn't thank them, though. Instead, he sarcastically asked, "What kept you?" They responded with laughter.

Just like that, the Battle of Castle Itter was over. Allied war correspondents and photographers were running around getting interviews and pictures, while U.S. troops were securing the area. Captain Schrader formally handed custody of the French VIP's over to the U.S. Army. A totally-drained Captain Lee saluted and shook hands with Captain Gill; Major Kramers; and the commander of the 142nd Infantry Regiment, 36th Infantry Division, Colonel George E. Lynch. The French were happily reunited with Zvonimir Čučković and Andréas Krobot and hailed them as heroes.

According to Schrader:

> "Borotra, who had managed to get through to Wörgl, also came back with the Americans. He was accompanied by the Yugoslav concentration camp prisoner Zvonimir Čučković, who immediately jumped at me and shouted something like: "Well, Hauptsturmführer." He looked at me with rage, as if he wanted to kill me. But cook Andréas Krobot intervened and explained that I had stood up for the French with my life. I introduced myself to the American Colonel and again handed the French over to the Americans." 54

While four of the German defenders had suffered injuries during the battle, there was only one casualty - Major Josef "Sepp" Gangl. His troops were taken into captivity as a precaution but were all soon released. Major Gangl was able to keep the promise he had made to his men that they would survive the war. Unfortunately, he didn't.

Captain Lee was more than ready to rid himself of this constantly bickering group of French VIP's. As Colonel Coyle walked up to him around 4 p.m., Jack saluted and then sighed deeply saying, "Take them, Colonel, they're all yours."

Lee and the other soldiers left the castle and arrived in Wörgl just in time to hear a radio broadcast that all Germans troops in Europe's southern front had agreed to stop shooting at noon. The castle battle, therefore, had actually gone into four hours of overtime. None of the soldiers involved thought of asking for extra pay. They were just glad to have gotten out alive.

The Battle Timeline

4 a.m.

- Captain Lee is awakened by gunfire as the 17th Waffen-SS Panzer Grenadier Division begins its attack. The first Allied shots are fired by SGT William Rushford using the tank's .50 cal gun.

- PFC's Herbert McHaley and Alfred Worsham use the tank's .30 cal gun to suppress enemy fire coming from the top floor of a nearby Inn in Itter.

- Cpl William Sutton fires his M-1 rifle at Waffen-SS cutting through barbed wire & attempting to scale the castle wall with grappling hooks and ropes. They climb back down & flee.

8 a.m.

- One of the Allied German soldiers takes off down the ravine & into the forest, apparently defecting to the enemy. PFC Arthur Pollack, fires his BAR machine gun at him but misses.

- Sepp Gangl reports seeing approximately 150 SS-Waffen troops dismounting from a column of trucks. Two Wehrmacht soldiers & an Austrian resistance fighter join as reinforcements.

9 a.m.

- The main assault begins. The castle's glass windows are shot out & chunks of masonry fall all around. Gangl & Lee find a wounded friendly German soldier.

10:30 a.m.

- General Gamelin takes his morning constitutional while his room is destroyed by an enemy 88mm
- The "Besotten Jenny" is hit by anti-tank rounds & explodes. Technician Fourth Grade Bill Rushford who was inside repairing the radio escapes unharmed.

2 p.m.

- Major Gangl is killed by sniper fire while trying to protect Paul Reynaud.
- Jean Borotra volunteers to vault the castle wall & walk through enemy lines dressed in peasant garb to reach the 142nd Infantry Regiment.
- The defenders run out of ammunition & are readying for hand-to-hand combat. One of the enemy points his *panzerfaust* at the gatehouse.

4 p.m.

- American rescue troops converge on the castle. Approximately 100 Waffen-SS are taken prisoner. The rest are killed or escape into the mountains.
- SGT's William Elliot & Glenn Sherman are the first to reach the castle. Lee walks out to greet them. He doesn't thank them, though. Instead, he sarcastically asks, "What kept you?"
- Lee turns the VIP's over to Col Coyle saying, "Take them, Colonel, they're all yours."

Ch. 11 - The War is Over

Hans Fuchs served as Itter's mayor from 1968 to 1988. As a 12-year-old, he watched the castle being converted into a prison. "We saw everything from our school window," Hans recalled, "There was a double barbed-wire fence and floodlights so that the whole night was lit up like day." Two years later, he watched the battle from his family's farm. "There was machine gun fire for hours," he said. "We saw clouds of dust and smoke." That evening, once the fighting stopped, he ventured down towards the castle, likely without his parents' permission or knowledge. "The tank was still burning," he reported. "I saw how around 100 SS men were taken prisoner... They had to give up everything and were taken away on lorries (troop transport vehicles.)" 55

Meyer Levin described events after the battle:

> "In a few minutes, the Joes were through the town and up the castle bridge, where Captain Lee's tank still burned. Photographer Eric Schwab rushed into the castle ground, and a dapper civilian with a familiar slouch hat seized him and kissed him on both cheeks. It was Daladier. Lieutenant Lutten, Zoonimir, Major Kramers, and all the rest came piling into the place and everybody congratulated everybody on the last-minute escape. Both Reynaud and Gamelin told how they were going to write books explaining the last days of France. Jouhaux told about his plans to go to the United States and consolidate the AFL with the

CIO. De le Rocque busily tried to explain that he had never been a Fascist. Reynaud and Mme. Mabire went upstairs and jumped on the lid of a trunk, trying to get it closed. Cailliau, brother-in-law of General de Gaulle, told how he had been forced to undress in winter, riding three days, stark naked and unfed, on the train to Buchenwald. General de Gaulle's sister told how she had been forced to spend nights in stables, sleeping on straw. Reynaud told how he had spent months in solitary confinement in Orunienburg." 56

Even in the end, the VIP's were still trying to outdo each other. Major Kramers observed sarcastically, "Perhaps some of these people were as happy to be liberated from each other's company as they were to be liberated from imprisonment." 57

Now safely in Allied hands, the prisoners rushed upstairs to pack their belongings, their heavy trunks loaded on a cargo truck in preparation for departure.

Before leaving the castle, Schrader received a short note written by one of the prisoners, Augusta Bruchlen, mistress of Labor Leader Leon Jouhaux. It read:

> "SS-Hauptsturmführer Kurt Siegfried Schrader took over, on 4/4/45, the security of the French internees in Castle Itter. He remained with them during the German attacks".

Although the note was hardly effusive in its praise, Schrader passed it around so that the others could sign it, attesting to his role in the conflict. He was relieved that he would have something tangible to show the Allied authorities that described his role in the fight. He, in fact, asked every one of the VIP's to sign it, which they did.

According to Schrader:

> "This important document was signed by all the former French prisoners. I returned to my apartment with my family. Thank God, the fighting for Itter ended without any further incidents. I gave my description objectively. The inhabitants of the small village of Itter, among them the Catholic village clergyman Höck, congratulated me on my service to the French.
>
> Since I had little outside contact, I had to make my own decisions. The responsibility was not easy, and yet I gladly accepted it. I simply had to do it. I was happy about the outcome, if you can put it that way."
> 58

Levin was a sceptic. It seemed to him that Schrader was operating out of his self-interest. He commented:

> "His sudden switch of loyalty was, of course, a gamble on the future, when we finally liberated Itter, this SS man ran around from room to room, he

was sweating, begging the former prisoners – the French politicians and generals – to sign a paper testifying to his courageous participation in the battle on their side." 59

Edouard Daladier after the liberation of Itter Castle.
Courtesy Agence France-Presse

Most of the French VIP's were told that they should plan to travel to Innsbruck. Daladier recalled:

"We all moved down toward the tanks and the automobiles. The people from the village had gathered in the town square. Austrian flags were hanging from the windows. An old antiques dealer from Berlin who had taken refuge in the area with his daughter, told us, 'We have been liberated, too.' I noticed that Resistance fighters from Wörgl were there as well. At 7 p.m., we headed down to Innsbruck, free at last. We were shown to the command post of the general leading the 103rd Division, Anthony McAuliffe. That was the heroic division that had been surrounded in Bastogne. The general had, in fact, been on leave at the time in the United States. He immediately had himself flown back and parachuted into the middle of his troops. He greeted us in princely, kindly fashion and honored us with a candlelight dinner in his Tirolean villa." 60

They were then taken by plane to Paris. It wasn't a standard charter flight. Charles de Gaulle made his personal aircraft available to fly the former honor prisoners from Innsbruck to Paris. They arrived to cheering crowds on May 10.

The friendly Germans who helped defend the castle were temporarily sent to a prisoner-of-war camp for processing. They were soon released and given special recognition for the help they provided to the Allies. All the numbered prisoners, including Zvonimir Čučković and Andreas Krobot, were returned to their home countries. Schrader, because of his former involvement as an SS officer, was given a two-year prison sentence but granted an early release due to the help he provided at the Battle of Castle Itter.

Captain Lee was awarded the Distinguished Service Cross (shown on the following page):

Courtesy National Archives

The captain's citation reads as follows:

"The President of the United States of America, authorized by Act of Congress July 9, 1918, takes pleasure in presenting the Distinguished Service Cross to Captain (Calvary) John C. Lee, Jr. United States Army, for extraordinary heroism in connection with military operations against an armed enemy while serving with Company B, 23rd Tank Battalion, in action against enemy forces on 4 and 5 May 1945. Captain Lee's intrepid actions, personal bravery and zealous devotion to duty exemplify the highest tradition of the military forces of the United States and reflect great credit upon himself, his unit, and the United States Army.

Two Sherman tanks of the 23rd Tank Battalion of the U.S. 12th Armored Division under the command of Capt. John C. 'Jack' Lee, Jr., and anti-Nazi elements of the Wehrmacht under the command of Major Josef 'Sepp' Gangl, arrived at Itter Castle. Together the three groups repelled probes by SS reconnaissance elements throughout the night. The battle continued through the morning of 5 May, with a strong force of 100–150 SS pressing the attack until reinforcements from the American 142nd Infantry Regiment arrived around 4 PM that day." [61]

The end of the German Third Reich was made official the morning of May 7, 1945, at Allied Headquarters in Reims, France. General Alfred Jodl, German Army Chief of Staff, signed surrender documents for the U.S., Great Britain, Russia, and France. Shown below are American soldiers celebrating the momentous event:

Courtesy www.jbsa.mil

The Soviet command asked that the Act of Military Surrender, including minor alterations to the Reims accord, be signed at Berlin the following day. To the Soviets, the documents signed on May 8, represent the official surrender of the Third Reich.

The strange story of the Battle of Castle Itter was actually a precursor of what was to come after the war – a Germany with a split personality. The Potsdam Conference, held from July 17 to August 2, 1945 divided Germany into four military occupation zones. France was given the Southwest, Great Britain the Northwest, the United States the South, and the Soviet Union the East.

NATO, the North Atlantic Treaty Organization, was formed on April 4, 1949 as a deterrent to Soviet expansion. On May 23, 1949, the American, French, and British Occupation Zones were combined to establish West Germany. The Soviet Zone was renamed East Germany and was hostile to the other allied powers. On October 3, 1990, the two Germanies finally united after more than 41 years of being apart. Since then, the American-German relationship has been a solid one with the two countries playing a leadership role among western democracies.

Lee had a succinct summation of that improbable fight at Castle Itter. A few months before his death, he was asked by a reporter in Norwich how he felt about the long-ago incident. He thought about what seemed to be the absurd notion of American and German troops joined together to defend French hostages in a medieval Austrian castle in a battle against other German troops. The very premise still sounded too outlandish to be true. After a long pause,

Lee said, "Well, it was just the damnedest thing!" No one has said it better.

This story features some German soldiers who had the courage to fight against their own government. Of course, you can ask, "Why didn't they fight from the beginning?" and "Why did they wait until it was obvious their side was going to lose to suddenly develop a conscience?" Those are fair questions. It probably makes these people less heroic than if they had objected when the Nazis first assumed power. But whether they resisted from the beginning, in the middle, or the end, the point is that they resisted.

The German Resistance Memorial in Berlin (shown on the next page) pays tribute to those, both military and civilian, who died because they were willing to stand up to the Nazis. It has a plaque that reads, "You Did not Bear the Shame, You Resisted, Sacrificing Your Life for Freedom, Justice and Honor."

Photo courtesy of Trip Advisor

After the War

Here's what happened to this story's main characters:

- **John C. "Jack" Lee Jr.**

Upon returning to the United States. Lee joined the Army Reserves. He went on to become a professional football player for several seasons with the New Jersey Giants, a minor league football team of the American Association, which folded in 1950. He then became a local football coach and a bartender. His personal life deteriorated as he displayed symptoms of PTSD (Post-Traumatic Stress Disorder) and struggled with alcoholism. Lee ran for political office but lost the election and tried to start a hotel business but it also ended in failure. His wife divorced him and was granted custody of their son. He married a total of three times. Lee passed away on January 15, 1973 from alcohol poisoning. He was 54 years old.

- **Jean Borotra**

Jean Borotra continued to play tennis professionally until retiring in 1956. He and the other Musketeers were inducted into the International Tennis Hall of Fame in 1976. Borotra later became founder and president of the International Fair Play Committee which promotes sportsmanship in competition around the world. Borotra and his wife, Mabel de Forest, divorced in 1947. In 1988, he married Janine Bourdin. As has been mentioned, he passed away on July 17, 1994 at the age of 95.

- **Josef "Sepp" Gangl**

After the Battle of Castle Itter, Major Gangl was buried at a cemetery in Wörgl, Austria. Today he is regarded as a national hero in Austria for his efforts to aid the resistance and protect Austrian citizens during the last days of the war. He is considered a part of the German Resistance, a collection of thousands of German citizens who opposed or resisted Nazi rule. A street in Wörgl bears his name.

- **Kurt Siegfried Schrader**

After his early release from prison in 1947, Schrader was happily reunited with his wife and daughters. Together they moved to Münster, Germany where he worked as a bricklayer in his post-war life. In 1953 he was given a position in the Interior Ministry of the North Rhein-Westphalia Region, which he held until 1980. Schrader passed away in 1995 at the age of 75.

- **Sebastian Wimmer**

The former commandant of Castle Itter was captured by Allied troops weeks after the war ended. Wimmer was considered a war criminal for actions he committed with the SS during World War II. Several of the VIP's from Castle Itter intervened on his behalf, and he was released in 1949. He went back to his hometown in Dingolfing, Germany in 1951. At this point, he struggled with alcoholism and his wife divorced him. Wimmer committed suicide on December 10, 1952 at the age of 50.

• **Paul Reynaud**

The former Prime Minister was elected to the Chamber of Deputies in 1946. He would later serve as the Minister of Finance and Economic Affairs. In 1949 he married his former

secretary Christiane Mabire, the prisoner who wrote the letter given to Zvonimir Čučković, that helped the Allies reach Castle Itter. They went on to have three children. Reynaud passed away on September 21, 1966 at the age of 87.

• **Edouard Daladier**

The former Prime Minister returned to France and continued to remain active in politics. He became a member of the Chamber of Deputies and went on to serve as mayor of Avignon from 1953 to 1958. He passed away on October 10, 1970 at the age of 86.

• **General Maurice Gamelin**

In 1946, the former Chief-of-Staff for the French Armed Forces published his memoirs entitled "Servir," which details his experiences in both World Wars. The decorated French General passed away on April 18, 1958 at the age of 85.

• **General Maxime Weygand**

Five days after his liberation from Castle Itter, the Free French Government arrested the former Chief-of-Staff for collaborating with the Pro-Nazi Vichy French Government. The disgraced general was eventually acquitted in 1948 and went on to write a number of books about his experiences. He passed away on January 28, 1965 at the age of 98.

• **Leon Jouhaux**

After the war Jouhaux resumed his role as president of the CGT (General Confederation of Labour.) He would go on to marry his mistress and one of the VIP prisoners, Augusta Bruchlen, in 1948. He later broke with the organization due to increased Communist influence and formed a democratic General Confederation. His work led to the creation of the ILO (International Labour Organization,) which is now part of the United Nations. In 1951, Jouhaux was awarded the Nobel Peace Prize for his work. He passed away on April 28, 1954 at the age of 74.

• **Francois de La Rocque**

After his liberation, the leader of the right-wing Croix de Feu wrote a book titled "Au service de l'avenir" (Serving the Future). He passed away on April 28, 1946 at the age of 60 due to complications from surgery for injuries he had suffered while serving in the French Army during World War I.

- **Marie-Agnes Cailliau**

The experience of being incarcerated haunted Marie-Agnes and her husband Alfred for many years afterwards. He was plagued by physical and psychological health issues until his death in 1956. In recognition for her service to the French Resistance in World War II, Marie-Agnes was awarded the Legion of Honour in 1975. Her book, "Souvenirs Personnels" or "Personal Memories" was published after her death on March 25, 1982. The sister of Charles de Gaulle was 93 at the time of her passing.

- **Michel Clemenceau**

The son of former Prime Minister Georges Clemenceau served as a member of the French National Constituent Assembly from 1946 to 1951. He passed away on March 4, 1964 at the age of 91.

- **Zvonimir Čučković**

After the war, the handyman returned to Yugoslavia where he set up an electrical business in Belgrade. He kept in contact with several former French POW's from Castle Itter, including Augusta Bruchlen-Jouhaux. He provided his accounts of life at Castle Itter, which she incorporated into her book *Prison pour hommes d'Etat* or "Prison for Statesmen." He passed away in 1984 at age 75.

- **Andréas Krobot**

Krobot seemed to disappear after the war, part of the wave of refugees across Europe. However, Mayor Hans Fuchs, reported that Krobot returned to Itter on holiday in 1974 and reminisced with him about his role in the battle.

- **Castle Itter**

The castle has once again passed into private hands and is not open to the public. The damage done to it in World War II has long since been repaired. There's no statue or public monument to the battle and the surrounding forest has grown to the point that the castle is barely visible from the road. Occasional tourists are disappointed that a "No Trespassing" sign is now at the very spot where the "Besotten Jenny" once stood guard.

"The Last Battle"

In 2017, the 12th Armored Division Association's "Hellcat News" published the lyrics of a song about the Battle of Castle Itter. It was part of an album released the previous year by German publisher Nuclear Blast, Red Distribution. The song is called "The Last Battle" from a Swedish group named Sabaton. Hellcat News also posted this warning - "Don't play it in the office…it is, after all, a power metal band." Here are the lyrics:

> "5th of May, V-day's just around the corner
> 1945, the Fuhrer's reign is at an end
>
> Jenny's at the gate, as the SS open fire
> There's no time to waste, the final battle's begun
>
> After the downfall, a castle besieged
> Facing the Nazis, awaiting relief.
>
> Gangl and Lee and their men set the prisoners free
>
> And it's the end of the line of the final journey,
> Enemies live in the past!
> And it's American troops and the German army
> Joining together at last!
>
> One last fight, it's the death throes of the Third Reich.
> Justice shall be done, the final battle remains.

Ammo's running low, they're depleting their machine guns.
Every bullet counts until the surrender's announced.

After the downfall, a castle relieved
Defeating the Nazis who had them besieged.
Gangl and Lee and their men set the prisoners free.

And it's the end of the line of the final journey,
Enemies live in the past!
And it's American troops and the German army,
Joining together at last!

(solo)
From the foot of the Alps to the shores of the sea…
From the foot of the Alps to the shores of the sea…
From the home of the brave, from the land of the free!
From the foot of the Alps to the shores of the sea…

And it's the end of the line of the final journey,
Enemies live in the past!
And it's American troops and the German army,
Joining together at last!
And it's the end of the line of the final journey,
Enemies live in the past!
And it's American troops and the German army,
Joining together at last!" 62

About the Author

Formerly a consultant who delivered more than 3,000 leadership and professional skills training seminars for many of the Fortune 100 companies and an Adjunct Professor at Boston University's School of Management, Len Sandler holds a B.S. in Psychology, an MBA, and a Ph.D. in Organizational Behavior. He is now retired and lives in Plymouth, MA with his wife Marilyn and dog Toby.

Len is the author of:

- *The Centennial Scandal: The Election of 1876*

- *Becoming an Extraordinary Manager: The Five Essentials for Success*

- *See You on the High Ground: The Jared Monti Story*

- *Because of You We Live! The Untold Story of George & Simone Stalnaker*

- *Mind Your Own Business: How to Jump-Start Your Career!*

Footnotes

1. Fest, Joachim C., *The Face of the 3rd Reich, Portraits of the Nazi Leadership*, Da Capo Press, 1999, p. 3.

2. https://www.goodreads.com/quotes/137599-if-you-win-you-need-not-have-to-explain-if-you Downloaded 12/9/22

3. Fest, 1999, p. 111.

4. https://www.goodreads.com/author/quotes/820213.Heinrich_Himmler. Downloaded 10/11/22.

5. Levin, Meyer, *Sat. Eve. Post, We Liberated "Who's Who."* July 21, 1945, p. 98.

6. Daladier, Edouard and Daladier, Jean, *Prison Journal 1940-1945*, Routledge, 2019, p. 317.

7. Levin, 1945, p. 17.

8. Daladier, 2019, p. 318.

9. Charles River Editors. *The Battle of Castle Itter: The History of World War II's Strangest Skirmish*, Kindle Edition, p. 29.

10. Rice, Bernard L., Indiana Magazine of History, *Recollections of a World War II Combat Medic,* December, 1997, p. 334-335.

11. Daladier, 2019, p. 318.

12. Harding, Stephen, *The Last Battle*, Hachette Books, Kindle Edition, 2013, p. 103-104.

13. Harding, ibid, p. 104-105.

14. Harding, ibid., p. 93.

15. Harding, ibid., p. 94.

16. Levin, 1945, p. 17.

17. Levin, ibid, p. 18.

18. Paul Reynaud *"Saved From Nazis at Castle Itter."* The Winnipeg Tribune. Winnipeg, Manitoba, Canada, August 11, 1945, p. 2.

19. Reynaud, ibid.

20. Reynaud, ibid.

21. https://www.historyofthewaffenss.com/community/main-discussion/battle-for-castle-itter-ss-hauptsturmfuhrer-kurt-siegfried-schraders-memoir, 1945. Downloaded 11/16/22.

22. Schrader, ibid.

23. Schrader, ibid.

24. Schrader, ibid.

25. Reynaud, 1945, p. 3

26. Harding, 2013, p. 94.

27. General Orders 33, HQ 12th Armored Division, U.S. Forces – European Theater, April 19, 1945.

28. https://www.12tharmoreddivisionmuseum.com/_files/ugd/c0865a_7bb533e7786a4a41b0e9bb2109f2ca06.pdf   Downloaded 10/15/22.

29. Schrader, 1945.

30. Levin, 1945, p. 98.

31. Daladier, 2019, p. 318.

32. https://www.12tharmoreddivisionmuseum.com/_files/ugd/c0865a_7bb533e7786a4a41b0e9bb2109f2ca06.pdf   Downloaded 10/15/22.

33. Schrader, 1945.

34. Levin, 1945, p. 18.

35. Schrader, 1945.

36. Levin, 1945, p. 98.

37. Daladier, 2019, p. 338.

38. Harding, 2013, p. 147.

39. Reynaud, 1945, p. 2.

40. Reynaud, ibid.

41. Levin, 1945, p. 98.

42. https://militarywiz.tumblr.com/post/116582883769/castle-itter-the-strangest-battle-of-ww-ii. Downloaded 12/3/22.

43. Daladier, 2019, p. 335.

44. https://www.tennismajors.com/atp/july-17-1994-the-day-tennis-legend-jean-borotra-passed-away-428632-html. Downloaded 9/22/22.

45. https//www.tennisfame.com/hall-of-famers/inductees/jean-borotra. Downloaded 9/15/22

46. https://www.tennisabstract.com/blog/2022/02/08/the-tennis-128-no-126-jean-borotra.

47. tennis abstract, ibid.

48. https//www.tennisfame.com/hall-of-famers/inductees/jean-borotra. Downloaded 9/15/22

49. https://www.quoteslyfe.com/quote/The-only-possible-regret-I-have-is-697935.

50. Mayer, John, Co. B, 23rd Tank Battalion, 12th Armored Division in *Hellcat News*, Vol. 3, No. 2, May 26, 1945.

51. https://www.militarywiz.tumblr.com/post/116582883769/castle-itter-the-strangest-battle-of-ww-ii. Downloaded 12/3/22

52. https://web.archive.org/web/20130719000400/http://www.lonesentry.com/newspapers/12tharmored.

53. Reynaud, p. 2.

54. Schrader, 1945.

55. https://www.bbc.com/news/world-europe-32622651?fbclid=IwAR0vnPj8wRfyKBjJI4Dk936jgiL_zVdd5_Uz36J7SCxx6ZtJLLe_AX6b-zE. Downloaded 12/6/22.

56. Levin, 1945, p. 18.

57. Levin, 1945, p. 98.

58. Schrader, 1945.

59. Levin, 1945, p. 18.

60. Daladier, 2019, p. 339.

61. General Orders No. 212, HQ 12th Armored Division, U.S. Forces – European Theater, General Orders No. 212 (1945)

62. Twelfth Armored Division (U.S.), *Hellcat News* (Garnett Valley, PA), Vol. 70, No. 9, Ed. 1, May 2017, P. 22.

Bibliography

Alexander, Martin S. *The Republic in Danger: General Maurice Gamelin and the Politics of French Defence,* 1933–1940. Cambridge University Press, 1992.

Bachinger, Eleonore; McKee, Martin; Gilmore, Anna; *Tobacco policies in Nazi Germany: not as simple as it seems*, PubMed, 2007.

Bear, Ileen, Adolf Hitler: A Biography, Alpha Editions, 2016, Kindle Edition.

Bischof, Günter, Fritz Plasser, and Barbara Stelzl-Marx, eds. *New Perspectives on Austrians and World War II*, Transaction Publishers, 2009.

Borrowman, Jerry. *Why We Fought: Inspiring Stories of Resisting Hitler and Defending Freedom*, Shadow Mountain, 2021, Kindle Edition.

Charles River Editors, *The Battle of Castle Itter: The History of World War II's Strangest Skirmish*, 2021, Kindle Edition.

Daladier, Édouard. *Prison Journal,* 1940–1945. Boulder: Westview Press, 1995.

de La Rocque, François. *Disciplines d'Action*, Parti social français, 1941.

Demey, Evelyne. Paul Reynaud, *Mon Père*. Plon-Opera Mundi, 1980.

Ferguson, John C., *Hellcats: The 12th Armored Division in World War II*. Abilene State House Press, 2004.

Francis, Jim. *A History of the 23rd Tank Battalion,* 1943–1945. Privately published, 2004.

"Freed – Daladier, Blum, Reynaud, Niemoeller, Schuschnigg, Gamelin," NY Times, May 6,1945, pg. 1

Harding, Stephen. The Last Battle: When US and German Soldiers Joined Forces in the Waning Hours of World War II. 2013.

Léon-Jouhaux, Augusta. *Prison pour hommes d'Etat,* Denöel/Gontheir, 1973.

Levin, Mayer, *We Liberated Who's Who*, Saturday Evening Post, July 21st, 1945.

Liszt, Franz, La Mara, and Constance Bache. *From Rome to the End: Letters of Franz Liszt*, Vol. 2, Icon Group International, 2008.

Long, Robert P. *Castle Hotels of Europe*, East Meadow, NY: Hastings House, 19
62.

Luza, Radomír V. *The Resistance in Austria, 1938–1945,* University of Minnesota Press, 1984.

MacDonald, Charles B., *European Theater of Operations: The Last Offensive. United States Army in World War II,* U.S. Government Printing Office, 1993.

Mayer, John G., *"12th Men Free French Big-Wigs."* 12th Armored Division, May 26, 1945.

Mitcham, Samuel W., Jr., *The Rise of the Wehrmacht: The German Armed Forces and World War II. Vol. 1*, Praeger Security International, 2008.

Mueller, Ralph, and Jerry Turk, *Report After Action: The Story of the 103d Infantry Division,* Battery Press, 1987.

Padfield, Peter, *Himmler: Reichsführer-SS*, Lume Books. Kindle Edition, 2020.

Pogue, Forrest C., *European Theater of Operations: The Supreme Command. United States Army in World War II,* U.S. Government Printing Office, 1954.

Reynaud, Paul, *In the Thick of the Fight,* 1930–1945. Translated by James D. Lambert. New York: Simon and Schuster, 1955.

Singer, Barnett. *Maxime Weygand: A Biography of the French General in Two World Wars*, McFarland, 2008.

Smyth, Sir John, *Jean Borotra, the Bounding Basque: His Life of Work and Play,* Stanley Paul, 1974.

Stein, George H., *The Waffen SS: Hitler's Elite Guard at War*, 1939-1945, Cornell University Press, 1966.

Sydnor, Charles W., *Soldiers of Destruction: The SS Death's Head Division,* 1939–1945. Princeton University Press, 1990.

Turner, Barry. *Countdown to Victory: The Final European Campaigns of World War II*, William Morrow, 2004.

von Steiner, Kurt. Resistance Fighter: Anti-Nazi Terror Tactics of the Austrian Underground, Paladin Press, 1986.

Digital Resources

https://nationalinterest.org/blog/buzz/us-and-nazi-soldiers-joined-forces-one-world-war-ii-battle-83796. Downloaded 11/5/22.

https://warhistoryonline.com/war-articles/the-battle-for-castle-itter.html?edg-c=1. Downloaded 10/11/22.

https://warriormaven.com/history/the-story-of-how-nazi-soldiers-and-the-u-s-military-once-fought-side-by-side-1. Downloaded 12/14/22.

https://texasmilitaryforcesmuseum.org/36division/archives/seigfri/freed.htm. Downloaded 8/16/22.

https://atlasobscura.com/places/castle-itter. Downloaded 9/26/22.

https://quora.com/What-was-the-story-behind-the-strange-battle-of-Castle-Itter-in-World-War-II%20. Downloaded 11/5/22.

https://.dailykos.com/stories/2019/4/30/1849004/-Hidden-History-Castle-Itter-When-Americans-and-Nazis-Fought-on-the-Same-Side. Downloaded 9/14/22.

https://gunsamerica.com/digest/major-josef-sepp-gangl-the-wehrmacht-hero-who-died-fighting-for-the-allies. Downloaded 10/5/22.

https://thevintagenews.com/2016/08/22/priority-19/?edg-c=1&A1c=1. Downloaded 10/14/22.

https://sofrep.com/news/battle-of-castle-itter-when-germans-and-gis-fought-side-by-side. Downloaded 11/4/22.

https://notesinhistory.blogspot.com/2015/11/the-strangest-battle-of-wwii-when.html. Downloaded 8/17/22.

https://wearethemighty.com/articles/that-time-when-americans-and-germans-fought-together-during-world-war-ii. Downloaded 10/11/22.

https://historycollection.com/six-facts-one-daring-missions-world-war-ii-battle-schloss-itter. Downloaded 7/18/22.

https://historia.id/militer/articles/aliansi-amerika-jerman-di-pertempuran-kastil-itter-vV9q1/page/1. Downloaded 9/7/22.

https://www.rallypoint.com/shared-links/fact-u-s-and-nazi-soldiers-fought-as-allies-once-during-world-war-ii. Downloaded 7/17/22.

https://militaryhistory.fandom.com/wiki/Battle_for_Castle_Itter. Downloaded 6/24/22.

https://www.thedailybeast.com/world-war-iis-strangest-battle-when-americans-and-germans-fought-together. Downloaded 10/8/22.

https://www.historynet.com/this-week-in-history-the-battle-of-castle-itter. Downloaded 11/5/22.

https://theunravel.com.au/the-battle-for-schloss-itter. Downloaded 6/8/22.

https://www.bbc.com/news/world-europe-32622651. Downloaded 10/3/22.

https://allthatsinteresting.com/battle-for-castle-itter. Downloaded 8/26/22.

https://transnationalhistory.net/doing/2018/02/26/a-croatian-electrician-two-army-officers-and-a-french-tennis-legend-toward-a-global-microhistory. Downloaded 7/12/22.

https://maximietteita.blogspot.com/2018/01/battle-for-castle-itter.html. Downloaded 4/17/22.

Made in the USA
Middletown, DE
06 March 2023

26104431R00086